WHEN GOOD PEOPLE

MAKE BAD

CHOICES

LARRY DUGGER

END GAME
Press

"Most people aren't trying to do the wrong thing—they just don't always know how to make good choices. In this book, Larry lays out very practical teaching on how to avoid some common pitfalls we can all fall prey to. After reading this book, I preached a sermon series based on the information and saw our church really increase in a desire to grow in the Lord. Larry takes important concepts of Christian growth and explains them in a way anyone can understand."
—Jamie Nunnally, Lead Pastor Victory Fellowship Church.

"People make bad choices. Buying Dugger's book is not one of them. In this book he provides hope for all who deal with regret and wonder if they've stuck with their self-made mess. By shining light on the stories of men and women in the Bible who committed their share (and then some) of bad choices, he helps his readers overcome their own ill-chosen actions. I highly recommend Larry Dugger's book."
—Mark Goodman, Lead Pastor, Rabbit Creek Church

"*When Good People Make Bad Choices: Overcoming Your Worst Decisions* hits the nail on the head. What our world is missing these days is truth in a firm yet loving way. Dugger does just that. He doesn't mince words about our bad decisions or how opportunities arise that give us the excuse to veer off track. Nor does he fail to show us how God's loving mercy can bring us back on the narrow path. A firm truth, unconditional love, and only God, who can mesh them all together. An excellent book to add to your library—one that can be pulled out and re-read again and again for the times we make another bad choice. A right-on read and a 100 percent must-have."
—Cindy K. Sproles, best-selling, award-winning author of *This is Where It Ends* and *Meet Me Where I Am, Lord*

"Many in the Body of Christ are proclaiming a message, projecting an image, and presenting a belief that followers of Christ should always succeed in everything they do. However, most of our experiences/realities tell a different story.

"Larry Dugger's latest book explores why believers struggle and brings us to the conclusion that it all comes down to the decisions we make. *When Good People Make Bad Choices* explores an in-depth look at why we make the decision we do, and what we can do to stop the cycle of failure.

"From my own experience, every bad choice I ever made led to a struggle with guilt and shame. Larry reminds us throughout this writing that there is good news, and that God has a better path, even when we make the wrong choice. In fact, when we have seemingly disgraced ourselves, God uses that disgrace as an opportunity to show us his grace!

"Every choice you make comes with a consequence, positive or negative. Larry helps the reader navigate the landmines in their thinking and teaches us how to avoid those same bad decisions in the future. He shows us how to recognize a bad decision BEFORE we have made it. That is a concept whose time has come for the Body of Christ.

"If you only read one book besides the Bible this year, let it be *When Good People Make Bad Choices*. You will see yourself in the intimate revelation Larry shares about his own struggles and failures, and you will be reminded that God does not reject you. Instead, like the biblical story of the Prodigal Son, the Father will welcome you back from those failures with open arms and a loving smile.

"Thank you Larry for the reminder to keep going."
—Dr. William Sharpless

When Good People Make Bad Choices

End Game Press books may be purchased in bulk at special discounts for sales promotion, corporate gifts, ministry, fundraising, or educational purposes. Special editions can also be created to specifications. For details, contact Special Sales Dept., End Game Press, P.O. Box 206, Nesbit, MS 38651 or info@endgamepress.com.

Visit our website at www.endgamepress.com.

Library of Congress Control Number: 2023951932
Hardback ISBN: 9781637972021
Paperback ISBN: 9781637971277
eBook ISBN:9781637972038

Cover by Dan Pitts
Interior Design by Dan Pitts

Published in association with Cyle Young of the Cyle Young Literary Elite, LLC.

Printed in the United States of America
10 9 8 7 6 5 4 3 2 1

To the staff at Family Church.
Each of you make me better. I love you all.

TABLE OF CONTENTS

INTRODUCTION

Let's face it—you've probably made some choices in the past you wish you could go back and change. I know I have. I'm not talking about finishing off the entire box of ice cream or the mullet that I sported in high school, even though, at the time, I thought it looked awesome. I mean the tough stuff. On more than one occasion, I've done or said something that brought serious fallout that I later regretted. Like Pandora, I opened a box full of consequences that spun my life out of control. The good news is, the bad decisions you and I sometimes make don't have to end in chaos or confusion. As unbelievable as it may sound, what if our mess ups are opportunities for us to learn and grow in our relationship with God? I believe they can be. Better yet, what if we could learn how to stop sabotaging our futures all together?

While a bad decision can create a topsy-turvy life, God has a better path. What you see as disgrace, God sees as an opportunity to show you His grace. He knows what to do with the things you wish you could undo. The Apostle Paul said it best: *"I really don't understand myself, for I want to do what is right, but I don't do it"* (Romans 7:15, NLT).

I can so relate to this scripture. I tangle with it more than I care to admit. I consider myself a reasonably mature Christian. I truly love Jesus. I go to church. I read the Bible on a regular basis. However, I occasionally act in ways that directly contradict my relationship with Christ. I don't always understand myself, either. You might be surprised to hear me say that, since I'm a pastor. But it's the truth. Perhaps there is more to the story. Paul goes on to say, *"For I know that nothing good dwells in me, that is, in my flesh. For I have the desire to do what is right, but not the ability to carry it out"* (Romans 7:18, ESV).

This verse often describes my life and, I am guessing, yours as well. While I always strive to make God smile with my actions, I sometimes catch myself struggling to make good choices as opposed to bad ones. God understands my dilemma and, in an effort to keep my life (and yours) on track, has left clearly defined guardrails in the scripture. He would rather I not drive off the cliff of bad decisions, but if I do, He is ready to catch me.

After more than thirty years of ministry, I've learned it's better to build a fence at the top of a cliff than a hospital at the bottom. The scripture is your guide when you are tempted to make a bad decision, establishing a clear path to avoid going over the cliff of a bad choice.

While others are quick to reveal your actions without explanation, the Bible gives a look inside the minds of those who embrace bad choices. Together we are going to learn from their mistakes and create a plan of action designed to take you forward.

As you move through the pages, you will see glimpses of yourself in each chapter. Some chapters will speak more loudly to you than others. This book is your survival kit. Keep it close. It serves as both a warning and a way out. Allow the material to either deliver you or fortify you against bad decision-making. Like Job's prayers, each page can become a hedge (Job 1:5), guarding against behavior that could potentially no longer be under the control of the Holy Spirit. Solomon offers this advice.

Above all else guard your heart, for it is the well spring of
life. Put away perversity from your mouth; keep corrupt

talk far from your lips. Let your eyes look straight ahead, fix your gaze directly in front of you. Make level paths for your feet and take only ways that are firm. Do not swerve to the right or to the left; keep your feet from evil (Proverbs 4:23-27, NIV).

The bad choices of your past only hold the power you continue to give to them. You're only one right choice away from making the next right choice. You can do this!

LUST

BURNING HOT

"As you yield freely and fully to the dynamic life and power of the Holy Spirit, you will abandon the cravings of your self-life"

(Galatians 5:16, TPT).

"Each of us is born with a box of matches inside but we can't strike them all by ourselves."

– Laura Esquivel, *Like Water For Chocolate*

It was just a spark. Nothing to worry about; after all, twin engines can handle sparks. A little flicker never crashed a plane. A mountain, maybe, that could take down a plane. A pilot, perhaps, on their first day of training, can bring down an airliner. Not a single spark.

Tell that to the families of the victims of ValuJet Flight 592. On May 11, 1996, what should have been a routine flight from Miami to Atlanta ended in a fiery blaze. The fire began in the cargo compartment. Improperly stored oxygen generators were the culprit. Sometimes a spark is all it takes.

Lust begins as a spark.

Like a spark, lust flickers low at first. No one pays much attention to a defective Fourth of July sparkler. There's nothing to see, right? We forget that sparks sometimes take down planes and people.

You may think you don't have a problem with lust; you might believe lust is more of a sexual sin. But let's think about it. When was the last time you were so obsessed with something it resulted in a bad choice? The designer handbag you can't afford, gaining the supervisor position at your job even though it would rob you of family time, or perhaps an unhealthy lifestyle that is slowly destroying your body. Lust is any out-of-control desire.

Tucked away in the book of 2 Samuel we find a story that is often overlooked. It is a prime example of what can happen when lust becomes an all-consuming monster. It also illustrates what you should do when tempted to pursue the wrong kind of passionate desire. In this Old Testament story, King David's beautiful daughter Tamar sparked the interest of her half-brother, Amnon. His infatuation with her was rooted entirely in lust. As a result of this unhealthy obsession, his life spun out of control as he made a string of bad choices. One bad decision can usually be quickly turned around, but when you continue down the path of bad choices, the consequences can be long-term and devastating. Let's look at where it all went wrong for this prince of Israel.

"Amnon became frustrated to the point of illness on account of his sister Tamar, for she was a virgin, and it seemed impossible for him to do anything to her" (2 Samuel 13:2, NIV).

We can only imagine Tamar's beauty. She came from the best stock in Israel. With every move she made, Amnon became increasingly aware of his all-consuming desire. Her virgin robe should have been a stop sign. Instead, the king's son could not take his eyes off his half-sister. Her presence left him frustrated and intoxicated. Lust was burning hot. Can you relate? Is there something you want so badly that it's driving you crazy, robbing you of sleep, or taking away your appetite?

Lust needs obsession.

A young prince, a middle-aged truck driver, or a retired teacher: it makes no difference. Lust is no respecter of persons. It flaunts what our flesh hungers for like a hot fudge sundae at the Weight Watchers meeting. Lust needs you to set your mind on something destructive and bad for you that your flesh is fixated upon. The writer of Romans gives us this warning,

"For to set the mind on the flesh is death" (Romans 8:6a, ESV).

Amnon had his mind set. Like a clock, where you set your mind determines where the hands go. Lust drove Amnon to the point of obsession. Tamar was all he could think about. Her scent, the way she glided through the castle, and the hair she pulled up in the summer, revealing the back of her neck, no doubt consumed him. His appetite for food was replaced by his appetite for Tamar. The small spark grew into an inferno.

Can you relate? Are you obsessed to the point of being sick about it? You yearn, crave, and desire something you know is not in your best interest. Are you in hot pursuit, only it feels like you're not the one driving? Lust likes to drive. Reckless and gas pedal to the floorboard, it's not afraid to commute.

My favorite bakery is located four hours from my home and if I'm being honest, there are days when that seems like a short distance. My desire for crème-filled chocolate donuts whispers, "Get in the car, Larry."

I think it's important to note that desire and passion aren't bad when they are pointed toward the things that breathe life into you. Passion can fuel your dreams and desire can motivate you to be your best. Lust for the wrong things, however, will motivate you to be your worst. Once an unhealthy desire emerges in your life, you can expect the enemy not only to identify that desire, but also to provide a plan of action designed to satisfy what your flesh is craving. This is exactly what happened to Amnon.

Lust needs a plan.

> Now Amnon had a friend named Jonadab son of Shimeah, David's brother. Jonadab was a very shrewd man. He asked Amnon, 'Why do you, the king's son, look so haggard morning after morning? Won't you tell me?' Amnon said to him, 'I'm in love with Tamar, my brother Absalom's sister' (2 Samuel 13:3-4, NIV).

After hearing Amnon's dilemma, Jonadab concocted a plan. "Go to bed and pretend to be sick," he said. "Tell your father it would make you feel better if Tamar cooked some food in your sight and fed it to you from her hand" (2 Samuel 13:5).

Lust needs a strategy to get what it wants. Amnon told his cousin, Jonadab, that he loved Tamar, but it wasn't love. Love is kind. Lust is conniving. Lust conspires and schemes. It survives in back-alley deals and under-the-table cover ups. Love protects the object of its attention. Lust feeds on it. That is the difference.

Jonadab said, "Get her alone. That will be your opportunity." Do you have a Jonadab? You know, someone in your life that makes you a lesser version of yourself. When lust is the problem, people like Jonadab must be avoided. Amnon was at a crossroads. Sick without her, but not brave enough to give in to his desire for her. All he needed was an extra push. Lust has friends and sometimes they are as close to you as cousins. All Amnon needed was a nudge. Who is nudging you?

That morning at breakfast, Amnon's choices were far more than just grape or strawberry jelly. (I would have chosen blackberry jelly.) He had to decide what to do with the lust that he felt for his sister. It's the same choice that you have when you're battling lust. Do you cross the line or stay on the right side of the line? Anytime you find yourself on the verge of giving in to temptation, the last thing you need to do is eat with a schemer. A nod of approval sounds like a starting pistol when lust is involved.

Keep in mind, even when you're following Christ, from time-to-time lust will show up at your front door. Bare shoulders, piles of cash, delicious desserts, recognition, and power pursuits will all find their way up the sidewalk to ring your doorbell. Their presence is not a result of God's absence, nor is it a result of your lack of spirituality. Lust hunted Jesus in the wilderness and lust will hunt you as well. It's natural and normal. You don't have to feel like a second-rate Christian when battling lust. Like Jesus, you must decide not to comply. Amnon, however, opened the door by creating the right environment to feed his flesh.

Lust waits for its opportunity.

"So Amnon lay down and pretended to be ill. When the king came to see him, Amnon said to him, 'I would like my sister Tamar to come and make me some special bread in my sight, so I may eat from her hand" (2 Samuel 13:6, NIV).

King David was not aware of his young son's intention. Without hesitation he sent his lovely daughter straight into the fire. Burning with passion, Amnon finally had his opportunity. Lust was no longer a spark; it was in full blaze.

Fittingly, Amnon wanted Tamar to prepare the food in his line of sight. Lust loves to look. Not with secret glances but with blatant glares. He can't take his eyes off her now. The very thing that he wanted most was now in reach. She kneaded the dough, he needed her. He watched. She baked. Lust grew.

Lust needs something to look at and fixate on. At this point, I want to be clear about exactly what I am saying. Lust isn't noticing someone you find attractive.

A few years ago, I received a phone call from a good friend. He was noticeably upset. He said, "Larry, every day when I am driving home from work, I see the woman who lives next door out jogging. I can't help but notice her and I feel terrible. What should I do?"

I said, "Unless you're circling the block to get a better look, I think you're okay." Even after you get married, you will still find certain members of the opposite sex attractive from time to time. It is normal and not a cause for concern. Lust, however, doesn't just notice; it fixates and is always positioning itself for a better view. Lust says, "I don't just want the bread. I want her to bake it in front of me." Job of the Old Testament gives great advice on the subject.

"I have made a covenant with my eyes; how then could I gaze at a virgin?" (Job 31:1, ESV).

A covenant is an agreement or a contract. In this case it is a contract that you make with yourself. Job said, "I have an agreement with my eyes. We're not looking." The decision was made in advance. This is important because where your eyes go, you soon follow. Keep in mind, it's not always a person lust is looking at. Lust looks at anything that causes an unhealthy infatuation.

Even though men tend to struggle more in the area of visual stimulation, women should also make this same covenant. In our culture of skin and more skin, this can be difficult. With the invention of the smart phone, we are marinating in pornography. While the internet is a wonderful resource, it is also a cesspool. The scantily clad are just a button's push away. It will be impossible for you to break the power of lust if you are unwilling to join with Job in his covenant. If the first glance is the spark, then the stare is the forest fire. The scenario with Amnon quickly heated up and began to burn out of control.

"Then Amnon said to Tamar, 'Bring the food here into my bedroom so that I may eat from your hand.' And Tamar took the bread she had prepared and brought it to her brother Amnon in his bedroom" (2 Samuel 13:10, NIV).

Lust is private.

Most of its participants are the least expected. A lawyer, a surgeon, and a prominent pastor often make the list. It needs us to go into the bedroom with it. After all, others cannot know. Approaching Tamar out in the open is something that Amnon would never do. It was too risky. Lust had a plan; now it needed privacy. The bed chamber of the young prince seemed like the perfect spot. Lust was ready to make a move. Do you have a private spot? Somewhere that you go so that others will not be aware of what you are doing?

"But when she took it to him to eat, he grabbed her and said, 'Come to bed with me, my sister" (2 Samuel 13:11, NIV).

The fantasy you entertained yesterday is working overtime to become your reality today. Lust had him before he had her. Lust made the first grab. Lustful thoughts are not a harmless way to deal with your stressful life, nor are they innocent and without consequence. This wasn't the first time he grabbed her. It was, however, the first time she was in the room with him. His intentions could not have been any clearer. He wanted to have sex with his sister. She, however, wasn't a willing participant. Tamar protested and begged Amnon not to force her. She reminded her brother of the shame and disgrace such an act of wickedness would bring not only to her, but also upon him (2 Samuel 13:12-13).

Lust exaggerates the payoff. "Go ahead. It will be fun," it says. "This is going to be better than you could ever imagine." All lies.

Tamar was right. Amnon was a fool, and his actions were wicked. Lust promises pleasure and delight but delivers pain and destruction.

Before we move on to the end of our story, I think it is important to clarify what I am communicating.

Sexual desire and arousal are not bad. In fact, they are very good. God created our bodies to do more than just procreate. He created us to enjoy the physical and emotional benefits of sex. Marital sex between a man and woman is God's gift. If you're looking for a great book filled with romance and lots of sex, I suggest you read the Song of Solomon. If sex is a fire, I like to think of marital sex as a controlled burn. It's safe, hot, and beneficial. In fact, I believe when God was searching for the perfect wedding present to give Adam and Eve, sex was on the top of the list. After all, it's the only gift you can continually open throughout your entire life and find it equally as exciting each time it's opened! Sex outside of God's law, however, is a wildfire that can potentially burn up an entire neighborhood.

The number of people who have been burned by lust continues to grow. The casualties are extensive. The flames of lust have taken more than their fair share of victims. Stop and think about the people in your life who have been victimized by lust, those who had no choice. Listen as Tamar pleads with Amnon.

"Please speak to the king; he will not keep me from being married to you.' But he refused to listen to her, and since he was stronger than she, he raped her" (2 Samuel 13:13b-14, NIV).

Lust turned a prince into rapist. Once ignited, the fire of lust destroys everything and everyone in its path. Tamar was the victim this time. She was helpless to fend off the advances of her lust-stricken brother. She paid the tab on what lust had ordered. Lust overpowers both predator and prey. Amnon invited the ravaging, Tamar did not. Amnon quickly found out that his out-of-control desire was setting him up for destruction.

Lust never delivers.

"Then Amnon hated her with intense hatred. In fact, he hated her more than he had loved her. Amnon said to her, "Get up and get out!" (2 Samuel 13:15, NIV).

This verse offers more evidence that Amnon's feelings were not love. Lust is temporary. If love never fails, then lust always fails. After lust gets what it hungers for, it disregards all attachment. Lust walks away wiping the corner of its mouth, pretending there was never a meal. What previously looked delicious is now casually pushed aside until the hunger pains start again. Lust is fleeting, yet always returns. Tamar was now nothing to Amnon and she wasn't ready to leave without telling him how disgraceful he had acted toward her.

She reminded him that sending her away would be even more disgraceful than what he had already done. Amnon, however, refused to listen. He demanded that his servants drag Tamar out, locking the door behind her (2 Samuel 13:16-17).

As was the case with Amnon, he did not want to face what he had done. Before he gave in to lust, he couldn't take his eyes off Tamar. Afterward, he couldn't stand to look at her. In fact, he was so adamant about getting rid of her that he had the doors bolted once she was gone. What he failed to realize was that there wasn't enough steel and wood in the entire kingdom to block what he had done. Lust believes if you can hide your behavior, no one will be the wiser. The problem with this theory is that where there is fire, there is also smoke. Tamar's full brother Absalom quickly learned all the sordid details. He waited for the perfect opportunity, and then two years later, he killed Amnon for what he had done.

Lust has consequences.

Absalom heard what happened to his sister. And he wasn't about to let Ammon get away with it. He had a plan—get Amnon drunk, and then kill him (2 Samuel 13:28).

Lust leads to death, with coffins full of marriages, ministries, money, and morals. It ends the same—a family standing on a canvas of manicured grass and plastic flowers, peering down a six-foot hole. You are there, looking up at them. The secret is out. You knew your actions wouldn't stay bolted behind bedroom doors forever, but you never expected this kind of fallout. The King of Kings knows about it. He always knew. Solomon was right.

"The eyes of the Lord are everywhere, keeping watch on the wicked and the good" (Proverbs 15:3, NIV).

Even though Amnon was able to hide his intentions from his father, King David, there was another King who saw the entire thing play out in heaven's movie theater. God watched as lust struck the match. Bolted doors are of little use when your King can see through walls.

Lust can be extinguished.

What if Amnon had extinguished the spark instead of fanning it into flame? What if he could have recognized the results of his actions before he acted? We will never know. It's too late. The princess has been raped and the prince is dead. This was no fairytale; however, it is a story that we should tell our children. Lust claims those on both sides. Perhaps we can look at this story with an eye for what should have happened. It didn't have to end in such tragedy. And while your life may be riddled with fallout, there is hope. This is not the end of your story! I propose three fire extinguishers that could have saved Amnon and without a doubt can save you.

1. Extinguish lust in your heart.

Our eyes may see, but our hearts feel. With every beat, our hearts race a little faster when chasing what we lust for. The addictions we so often feed and what Amnon felt for Tamar are the same. The pounding in Amnon's chest only reminded him of his out-of-control desire. When your heart is throbbing with lust, make sure to give it to the right person. Tamar didn't want Amnon's heart, but God did.

"My son, give me your heart" (Proverbs 23:26, ESV).

When your heart doesn't belong to God, it is often empty. Empty hearts are vulnerable hearts. Lust is looking to rent a room. It says, "Just for the night," but it always stays longer. I will not assume that every person reading this book is a Christian. Perhaps you've been considering the idea but haven't yet made the commitment. If so, I offer this advice, your willpower isn't nearly as effective as the Holy Spirit's power. If you want God's help, you must invite Him to help. Before you proceed, pray if you feel prompted.

"Lord Jesus, I believe that you died on the cross for my sins. All of them, including lust. I invite you into my heart and ask for your forgiveness. Help me to live for you from this day forward, in Jesus' name. Amen."

Once your heart belongs to God, you're still responsible to keep it clean. Like brushing your teeth, keeping your heart clean is not a one-time deal. It is daily. Christian hearts become vulnerable when we treat our spiritual leaders like the maid in charge of doing the cleaning instead of taking personal responsibility to keep our hearts clean ourselves. David knew. In one of his most famous Psalms, he tells God of his need for a clean heart (Psalm 51:10). Lust loses its power when we are diligent in our spiritual hygiene. Amnon talked to Jonadab about the dirt in his heart; you should talk to Jesus about the dirt in yours. Jonadab offered release. Jesus offers rescue. Jonadab said, "Go to her." Jesus says, "Come to me."

Never be afraid to talk to Jesus about Tamar. I will let you in on a little secret, He already knows all about her. Telling Him will come as no surprise. Invite Him into the dirt. He will come and He will bring a M.O.P. (More Overcoming Power!)

2. Extinguish lust by fleeing from it.

If you don't want a lion to pick his teeth with your bones, then stay out of his den. Ironically, there is an adult entertainment business called the Lion's Den near my home. When driving by, I can't help but wonder how many victims never made it out. Amnon should have stayed out of the bedroom. The Apostle Paul understood how powerful lust can be and gave his young apprentice, Timothy, this piece of advice.

"But flee youthful lusts, and follow after righteousness, faith, love, and peace, with them that call on the Lord out of a pure heart" (2 Timothy 2:22, ASV).

When lust is involved, run for your life. Nowhere in the Bible are we ever encouraged to stay in the same room with lust. We can stand on the promises of God, but standing with lust is not wise. Making a quick exit is always more effective than trying to prove how spiritual you are by standing toe-to-toe with seduction. You should avoid any situation that might cause you to compromise. You don't have to prove how spiritually strong you are by taking Tamar into the bedroom and then refusing to act on your lustful thoughts. Make a run for it! It's not cowardly, it is courageous. We battle lust by simply not being there. Removing yourself from the environment of compromise is key.

3. Extinguish lust by taking it to the king.

Tamar said something profound that we cannot overlook. When Amnon was under the sway of lust, she recognized the answer. She said it without realizing how spot on she was.

"Don't do this wicked thing ... Please speak to the king" (2 Samuel 13:12-13, NIV).

She was convinced that King David would give her to Amnon as a wife. She saw the king as being an answer to the problem. May I suggest that the King is still the answer? Not King David but the King of Kings. Where do you take your lust? Do you go to the throne room or the bedroom? Are you like Amnon? Are you refusing to listen?

"But he refused to listen to her, and since he was stronger than she, he raped her" (2 Samuel 13:14, NIV).

Lust doesn't want to talk to the king. The king is the last thing on its mind. Stronger and more powerful than those victimized, lust pushes forward without regard for the inevitable outcome. Tamar was right. Consulting the king was a better choice. He of all people would understand how powerful lust could be, and no doubt tragedy could have been avoided. Amnon had no plan other than to give in to his lust. If he had spoken to the king, the consequences of moving forward would have been spelled out for him. Before lust grabs you, before unbridled passion takes over, yell for the King!

Wrapping it up.

Lust is a formidable opponent. It wrestles in all weight classes. No one is exempt. Both priest and prostitute are invited to the fight. Those who stay in the ring, rather than call on the King, don't last long. Amnon lost his life. If you're reading this, you still have yours. Make no mistake, you will not get out unscathed. Something will die. Perhaps it will be your marriage, reputation, finances, health, a job that you love, or even your ministry. Lust wants everything that you hold dear. In the same way that you crave whatever it is that you're obsessed with, lust is obsessed with your future. Lust is hungry for the good days ahead of you. If left unchecked, it will consume them.

Perhaps you already know this. It is not new information. You're a professional. Tamar gets dragged from the dining room to the bedroom and back to the dining room daily. It's getting harder for you to hide what you're always preoccupied with. You're exhausted. You need help, don't you? I have provided you an example of lust and a plan for dealing with it. Now the choice is yours. Do you continue down the road paved by lust, or do you take the high road and decide to get better? Do you ignore the King or speak to Him about your problem? What will you do?

You have probably said that you're sorry at least a thousand times, but a thousand apologies haven't been enough to make you stop. Right? It's time to stop being sorry and start owning your behavior by changing it. You need deliverance. I find it interesting that in The Lord's Prayer, Jesus teaches his disciples to approach God specifically concerning their behavior.

"And lead us not into temptation, but deliver us from the evil one" (Matthew 6:13, NIV).

This is a prayer that needs to once again be shouted from the rooftops. Let's start by shouting it from wherever you're reading this book. Go ahead. It is okay. Aggressive sin calls for an aggressive response. Shout it. "Deliver me from evil." Louder. "Deliver me from evil." Again!

Let it go. Let it spill out like the poison in a festered blister. Take a minute and speak to the King. Use your own words. Talk with tears if you must. Tell Him what you have done and what you're going to do about changing it. Take your time. This prayer will help,

"Lust, release me in Jesus' name. I refuse to be controlled by your appetite for destruction. I renounce every unruly thought, motive, and behavior. From this day forward I choose to walk in the Spirit and no longer be ruled by my flesh. Lord, give me the strength to stay away from every person, place, and situation that stirs up lust in my heart, in Jesus' name, Amen."

REFLECTION QUESTIONS

1. Identify the people, places, and things that stir up lust in your heart. How will you invite God's help into those places of weakness?

_____

_____

_____

_____

_____

_____

"Create in me a pure heart, O God, and renew a steadfast spirit within me" (Psalm 51:10, NIV).

2. Passion and desire can be positive when pointed in the right direction. How will you use the hunger God has placed inside of you to achieve your goals?

_____

_____

_____

_____

_____

_____

"My soul longs, yes, faints for the courts of the Lord; my heart and flesh sing for joy to the living God" (Psalm 84:2, ESV).

3. Lust can be a result of poor spiritual hygiene. Examine your daily walk with God. How are your prayer life, Bible study habits, and church attendance? Do you need to make changes?

_____

_____

_____

_____

_____

_____

"My council for you is simple and straightforward: Just go ahead with what you have been given. You received Jesus Christ, the Master, now live in him. You're deeply rooted in him. You're well-constructed upon him. You know your way around the faith. Now do what you have been taught. School's out; quit studying and start living it! And let your living spill over into thanksgiving" (Colossians 2:6-7, MSG).

WILD LIVING

BREAKING BAD

"Not long after that, the younger son got together all he had, set off for a distant country and there squandered his wealth in wild living"

(Luke 15:13, NIV).

"May the things of this world so lose their power over us that we do not in the slightest wish to be worldly."

– Watchman Nee

What comes to mind when you hear the word worldly? To me, it just sounds "churchy." After all, the cashier at the Quick Stop never asks if you're feeling worldly today! In my opinion the term is often misunderstood, but it doesn't have to be.

Simply put, worldliness is a willful walking away from God to pursue what He will not be a part of. The world doesn't know it's worldly, but a follower of Jesus should. The world is more than just the Earth we live on. It's an attitude that excludes God from your life. Many have walked this path only to find out it wasn't what they anticipated.

What if you had a plan of action that will keep you firmly rooted in your love relationship with God when wild living calls out to you? What if you could learn to put the Heavenly Father before every earthly pursuit? I believe you can! Guarding your faith is of the highest importance because you never spiritually arrive at a place where you're not tempted to push God aside for something else.

As a pastor and professional counselor, I regularly visit with those whom others consider spiritual giants, and yet even they sometimes find themselves sidelined by what the world is offering. While future chapters may or may not apply to your life now, this one will speak to you. Perhaps you're the one slowly slipping away from the Father. Or maybe someone close to you is making that mistake and you can use the information to aid their rescue. Even the most faithful sons and daughters of God sometimes wrestle with thoughts of leaving home. You must be on guard. The Apostle Paul gives this gentle reminder.

"No temptation has overtaken you except what is common to mankind. And God is faithful; he will not let you be tempted beyond what you can bear. But when you are tempted, he will also provide a way out so that you can endure it" (1 Corinthians 10:13, NIV).

This verse gives me great hope. I know that no matter what tempting situation I find myself in, God has already provided a way of escape. I don't have to be intimidated by my surroundings or what I'm facing. Paul was right. The God who lives in my heart has more power than the things trying to sway my heart.

In Luke 15, Jesus tells a collection of stories (or parables) about items that aren't lost, but somehow get lost. From coins to kids, He illustrates how easy it is for things to come up missing. Have you ever gone spiritually missing? You know, you were showing up for God and then you weren't? The world seeks to take you off the life path so that you get lost in the surrounding wilderness. You go in thinking you can easily find your way back; after all, you won't be gone long. However, you quickly realize getting out isn't as easy as you thought. Jesus used the story of a kid who got mixed up in the world to explain the dangers of wild living to His followers.

Wild living is a road to nowhere.

"Jesus continued: 'There was a man who had two sons. The younger one said to his father, 'Father, give me my share of the estate.' So he divided the property between them" (Luke 15:11-12, NIV).

Even though this story revolves around a rich landowner and his two boys, it perfectly illustrates the heart of our Heavenly Father. God doesn't keep hostages—not even for a day. I bet if heaven had bird cages, there would be no doors. Keep in mind: like the boy in our story, you're free to walk away from the Heavenly Father at any time, but you're not free of the consequences. The son's request was very unusual. Just image going to your parents, telling them you're moving to a place they don't approve of, and then asking them to pay for it! When the world calls, you have a choice. Listen and leave home with partial benefits still intact (for now) or stay and receive the full inheritance. The boy in this story chose to leave.

Wild living leads you away from the Father.

"Not long after that the younger son got together all he had, set off for a distant country and there squandered his wealth in wild living" (Luke 15:13, NIV).

Notice, he was still a son—he just wasn't acting like one at the time. Can you relate? I can. Are you sometimes tempted to step outside the values of your spiritual family? Like the young son, do you have days when you think you might want to leave the farm to explore parts of the world that are unknown to you?

I remember one counseling client I saw a few years back. He was a tall, handsome guitar player. Let's call him Jeff. He was raised by loving Christian parents who taught him to serve God above all else. When Jeff turned eighteen the world began calling to him, so he left home to pursue a totally different life path. It wasn't at all what he had anticipated.

He said, "I still thought about God every day, but my life looked nothing like Him. There were moments when my new lifestyle seemed exciting, but at night the emptiness always returned. I spent five years slowly circling the drain before realizing how much better my life was when pleasing God was my priority. God had not left me, but I had left Him."

As the proud father of two boys, it is difficult for me to imagine the scenario. I picture the dad in this story standing at the gate in front of the house. One of the gateposts is leaning slightly to the left. It has been well used. Cows have jumped it. Guests have crossed it. Today, his youngest boy would walk through it on his way to God-knew-where. Personally, I don't think I could have let him go, or at the very least, I would have gone with him. But not the father in this story. Like our Heavenly Father, he would not follow his son into disobedience. Here is why.

"Do not love the world or the things in the world. If anyone loves the world, the love of the Father is not in him" (I John 2:15, ESV).

Wild living refuses rescue.

The father loved the boy regardless; however, he did not offer rescue at the first sign of trouble. He waited until he was ready to come back home. No matter how long you've been a Christian, remember the world will never stop pursuing you. Wild living doesn't care if you're a son. The world has no regard for your inheritance or the consequences that come with wasting it on things of no real value. If you go, you will have to walk past the Father to get there.

At times we've all wasted our inheritance in one way or another. Problem is, a walk on the wild side leads to empty on the inside. Wild and reckless living will feed you until you're about to burst. One more bite, look, taste, and touch. And once fat with self-indulgence, it makes starving you that much sweeter. Jesus explains further.

"After he had spent everything, there was a severe famine in that whole country, and he began to be in need" (Luke 15:14, NIV).

Like his money, his friends were soon gone. The world always promises you a jackpot (otherwise no one would pay attention) and then takes it back with interest due. The young son could only reminisce about what he walked away from. I can see him looking up into the branches of a bare apple tree, thinking about the fresh apple pies sitting on the windowsill back at the farm. Everything that he had taken for granted was all that he wanted now. This would have been a great time to kiss the world goodbye and head for home, but he didn't. He made the same mistake that a lot of us make. He decided to keep pushing forward without the father.

Wild living creates its own problems.

"So he went and hired himself out to a citizen of that country, who sent him to his fields to feed pigs. He longed to fill his stomach with the pods that the pigs were eating, but no one gave him anything" (Luke 15:15-16, NIV).

Fattening the calf (Luke 15:23) for his father was one thing, but to fatten an unclean pig was worse. To top it off, his boss wouldn't even let him eat the pig food. Like the pigs he was tending, wild living cakes you in mud. The dirt he stirred up was now holding him securely in the pig pen. Does that sound familiar? That is precisely how worldliness works. Knee deep in what he had done, he felt trapped with the pigs of poor choices. This is the path you must avoid.

Jesus also dealt with pigs. On one occasion He even cast a legion of demons into a herd of them. The pigs then ran off a steep cliff, fell into a lake, and drowned, committing "sooey-cide" (Luke 8:32-33). To me that seems harsh. After all, what did the innocent pigs do?

I believe Jesus was teaching a lesson. Often we want Jesus to take care of our demons. We want Him to put them in pigs, put them somewhere. We no longer want to deal with them. The problem is, after Jesus puts our demons in the pigs, we want to keep the pigs! We want the pigs around just in case we might want to return to the wild behavior in the future. Jesus got rid of the pigs. Just like the boy in this story, the day must come when you are ready to say, "Goodbye, pigs!" Maybe someone has even said to you, "I will believe you've changed the day pigs fly." Let them fly!

Wild living doesn't want you to come to your senses.

"When he came to his senses, he said, 'How many of my father's hired men have food to spare, and here I am starving to death!'" (Luke 15:17, NIV).

The first step home started with both feet still planted firmly in the pig pen. There was something happening in the mind of our young perpetrator. He grew tired of being conformed to the world and was being transformed by thoughts of home (Romans 12:2). His mind made the journey before he did. I think it is worth noting that the trip to the pig pen happened in the same manner, only in reverse. With both feet planted in the father's house, his mind began to conjure images of a life without the father's approval. Keep in mind, your behavior is just your thoughts turned inside out. Like a dirty sock casually tossed in the laundry basket, it is hard to identify the dirt until you reach in and pull it right side out. Wild living reaches into your thought life hoping to find some dirt. The prodigal began fixing his life by fixing his thoughts. The same is true for you as well. His plan was simple—return wholeheartedly back to the father.

Convinced that his son-status was a thing of the past, the young man had an idea. If he could no longer be a son, maybe he could be a servant (Luke 15:18-19). All he wanted was to move back home, even if it meant sleeping in the barn.

Perhaps you're reading this chapter and finding it hard to identify with the young son. After all, you never left the farm and have no intention to. Let's consider the older brother for a moment. Maybe there is a lesson here as well.

I can just hear big brother. "Dad, why do you spend so much time standing at that gate? He is not coming back. It's been months since he left. I don't even know why you care anyway. You've heard the rumors. He's gone wild. He's ruined our family name!"

I can see big brother walking off, kicking up dust, and mumbling under his breath. If his little brother did muster enough nerve to come home, he'd give him a piece of his mind. Word of his outrageous behavior had reached the church. (I mean the farm.) If his father wasn't going to handle him, he would. Wild living loves it when big brother is in charge. Pastor Big Brother, Deacon Big Brother, or even Christian Big Brother, it doesn't matter. Those who are experimenting with the wild side of life stand little chance of returning when Big Brother guards the gate. They need a dad like the one in our story at the door.

Wild living can't overcome the urge to return home.

"So he got up and went to his father. But while he was still a long way off, his father saw him and was filled with compassion for him; he ran to his son, threw his arms around him and kissed him" (Luke 15:20, NIV).

This dad was happy to have his boy home even though he still had the stench of where he had been in his clothes. Good dads don't care when our diapers are dirty. Wild living panics when the stink gets hugged out of us. The young man said, "I am no longer worthy to be your son. I have sinned against you."

The words barely had time to slide out of the boy's mouth, when the father did something unexpected. He brought out the best robe and put it on him. The father also slid a ring on his finger. "Bring out the fatted calf and let's have a feast," he declared (Luke 15:21-23).

Wild living can't compete with a compassionate father.

When he left the father, he was a son wearing shoes. When he returned from the world, he was a barefoot slave. That's how wild and reckless living works. Our rights as sons get left in the mud. The pig pen claims more than our shoes. Our identities also get lost in the muck. Wild living is hungry for the person you used to be. A son, faithful spouse, trusted employee, and celebrated pastor are just a few of the titles it seeks to devour. Compassion, however, knows the protocol. Slaves go barefoot, not sons.

He didn't deserve such a welcome home party. The shoes, jewelry, and robe came as quite a surprise. The father's final request, however, was beyond belief. "Kill the fatted calf." The boy knew about the calf. It wasn't like the others in the herd. It had been given special treatment from the time it was born. Big brother also had his eye on it (Luke 15:30). But the father was reserving it for a grand celebration. It was the choicest of their cattle.

Tears streaming and heart pounding, the boy fell to his knees. "The choicest of my father's cattle for my poor choices. I don't deserve this. The best for my worst? Father is obviously mistaken." The father explains the reasoning behind his request.

"'For this son of mine was dead and is alive again; he was lost and is found.' So they began to celebrate" (Luke 15:24, NIV).

The father wasn't concerned about the inheritance that the young son had wasted, nor did he care about the boy's blatant disregard for the family name. He was just glad his boy was home. Not everyone, however, shared in his enthusiasm.

Returning from wild living won't make everyone happy.

When the young son's older brother heard music and celebration coming from the house, he asked one of the servants what was going on. The servant told him of his little brother's return and how the father killed the fatted calf. This news angered the older brother and he refused to go inside (Luke15:25-28).

There will always be a big brother, someone whose memory of your shortcomings outweighs their enthusiasm over your return. Those who believe their obedience deserves more attention than your repentance. The father makes a strong case. "Your brother was dead and now is alive again." The father saw the big picture and we should as well. The son who stayed home was safe. The father could feed, care, and look after him. The son who left was very much on his own. The father was removed from the equation, not by his choice, but by the son's choice. It is no wonder the occasion called for such a lavish menu item. The son was home; that is all that mattered.

This story has already played out, but yours hasn't. What starts in your mind as a speck of dirt can grow into a mountain of mud. The once-stable boundaries of your life can give way to the mudslide. You can slide back to the pigs, but you don't have to. Wild living gives you more grime than glory. The best of us can become the homeless child of an extravagant father. Like the prodigal, you too may have broken bad. Or perhaps you're thinking of walking away just to see what is out there. Whatever the case, take heart; your mud is not too deep. You might have fallen, but you don't have to stay down.

"For though the righteous fall seven times, they rise again" (Proverbs 24:16a, NIV).

Even if you already feel the mud between your toes, you don't have to stay stuck in it. Wild living needs you to believe that you've exhausted all your chances. Rookie sinners and professional backsliders, the dirt wants them both. What wild living won't tell you is that Father is ready to welcome you back home. He doesn't care how long you have been gone or how many times you've gone before. Your room will always be just as you left it.

Wild living takes your identity; take it back.

He wasn't always the rebellious, broke, pig-feeding foreigner. No, he started as the clean-cut kid from the successful cattle farm across the county line. Wild living took more than his money. It took him. There are no mirrors in a pig pen. It's hard to see what you've become when you no longer care who you are. If only he could have seen what others saw, he might have made the trip home sooner.

The lost son was a diminished version of his former self. Wild living promises a new identity. The problem is that is exactly what you get. If you have already fallen into this trap, I have a question. Who did you used to be before the pig pen? You know, what was your title before the dirt took you down? Pastor? Married? Deacon? Virgin? Respected? Faithful? What did they used to call you? I am not trying to add insult to injury. I am just reminding you of the person we are looking for. There is someone at the door. I think it is you! Listen as John the Revelator explains your next move.

"Remember the heights from which you have fallen, and repent and do the things you did at first" (Revelation 2:5, AMP).

The lost son needed to go back home, and perhaps you need to as well. The people you have disappointed and damaged, like the older brother, may or may not be waiting for you at the gate. The Father, however, will be waiting. He is the one with whom you must make amends. He has been watching for you. Don't panic, He already knows what you smell like.

It's okay to cry. Don't worry about the mud on your face. Tears leave highways of flesh on a canvas of dirt. The dirt needs to go. Tears are the best soap. You're coming back to yourself. Aren't you? Your actions may have enslaved you, but you're not a slave. You're a son! Not just any son at that. The calf has been reserved for the day of your homecoming. The entire time you were gone, the Father never stopped feeding it. He fattened it, not for those who have never left, but for you. The Father values you above all else. You may have failed, but you're not a failure. Your identity is waiting for you to reclaim it. Your robe, slippers, and new ring are just more evidence of the Father's love for you. They are also proof that you can recover everything you lost when you left.

If you are ready to renounce friendship with the world, then it's time to pray. When dead slaves pray, live sons are resurrected. Pray with me. It's resurrection day.

"Father, I have sinned against heaven and against you. I am no longer worthy to be called your son." Welcome home, son.

REFLECTION QUESTIONS

1. Identify those areas where wild living calls out to you. How will you safeguard your life so that you don't accept the call?

_____

_____

_____

_____

_____

_____

_____

"Don't become so well-adjusted to your culture that you fit into it without even thinking. Instead, fix your attention on God. You'll be changed from the inside out. Readily recognize what he wants from you, and quickly respond to it" (Romans 12:2a, MSG).

2. After leaving the father, the prodigal son lost both his wealth and his self-worth. What does the world most often try and take from you? How will you take back what gets stolen?

_____

_____

_____

_____

_____

_____

_____

_____

_____

_____

"And from the days of John the Baptist until now the kingdom of heaven suffers violence, and the violent take it by force" (Matthew 11:12, NJKV).

3. Like the big brother in our story, sometimes we fail to demonstrate grace and mercy to those who make poor spiritual choices. Like the father, how will you be more merciful in the future?

_____

_____

_____

_____

_____

_____

_____

_____

"My beloved friends, if you see a believer who is overtaken with a fault, may the one who overflows with the spirit seek to restore him. Win him over with gentle words, which will open his heart to you and will keep you from exalting yourself over him (Galatians 6:1-2, TPT).

GOSSIP

THE DEVIL'S RADIO STATION

*"Listening to gossip is like eating cheap candy;
do you really want that junk in your belly?"*

(Proverbs 18:8, MSG)

"Gossip is the devil's radio station, so don't be his DJ."

– George Harrison

I destroy relationships, separate lifelong friends, annihilate reputations, and split churches. I get pleasure from half-truths and twisted facts. I speak in riddles, not realities. I go where you go. The store, park, gym, and beauty salon are only a few of my favorite hangouts. You can't even vacation without me. I am always along for the ride. I am everywhere.

My name is gossip.

It's usually not what happens in life that causes the most destruction, it's the retelling. The embellished story spreads. Like the plague, we can pass it around town. It grows as it goes. Before long, the story is more made up than spot on. Gossip has been around for as long as man has walked the earth. It's not the story that can't be kept straight, it's us. Regurgitating boring facts isn't nearly as appealing as adding juicy tidbits. We all do it to some degree—even me. You and I have a choice to make here. Will we be a part of the problem or the solution?

Maybe you have never considered yourself a gossip.

After all, you're just a concerned citizen, right? I mean, come on, others have the right to know when something fishy is going on. Don't they? I love to watch reruns of "The Andy Griffith Show." Sheriff Taylor and company make life in small-town America very appealing. Mayberry is somewhat of a utopia. It was a place where there was no need to lock your doors at night, and even the town drunk was more like a lovable uncle than a raging alcoholic.

Everyone in Mayberry appeared to have the best interest of others in mind. Aunt Bee is one of my favorite characters. She was the lovable saint who served her church and community in nearly every episode. Her interaction with her best friend, Clara, is something I find hilarious. These two pillars of the church community were constantly gossiping about their friends and neighbors. However, they always did it with an undertone of concern. In their minds, they weren't gossiping at all. The writers of the show did a fabulous job portraying how gossip is often disguised as concern. I mean, after all, it's not gossip if it's true, right? It's not really spreading rumors if you're genuinely concerned, is it? Um, yeah, it is.

Gossip is the devil's radio station. He is always looking for DJs. He needs someone who will report the news not as it is, but rather as they heard it—or interpreted it. A gossip takes the private details of someone's life and reveals them as sensational facts. It is often done under the guise of being worried about the person or even presented as a prayer request. A gossip says, "Please pray for Molly. You know her husband just kicked her out for sleeping with his best friend. I think his name is Fred. We should probably pray for Fred as well. You remember Fred. He is the Sunday school teacher at the church on the corner and works at Walmart."

Solomon believed that gossip exposes, but prayer covers.

"Whoever goes about slandering reveals secrets, but he who is trustworthy in spirit keeps a thing covered" (Proverbs 11:13, ESV).

A gossip reveals details about others that may or may not be true. They enjoy exposing the personal circumstances of friends, family members, neighbors, and even strangers. They are only concerned with who they're going to tell next. Gossip is the opposite of genuine concern and covers nothing. A trustworthy person, on the other hand, can be counted on to make sure that your business doesn't become everyone's business. They will not cover it up, but they will cover you up in prayer. We see this scenario playing out in the very first book of the Bible.

Gossip exposes the nakedness of others. It's a bed without covers.

"Noah, a man of the soil, proceeded to plant a vineyard. When he drank some of its wine, he became drunk and lay uncovered inside his tent. Ham, the father of Canaan, saw his father's nakedness and told his two brothers outside" (Genesis 9:20-22, NIV).

This was front-page news kind of stuff. The righteous, blameless boat builder who walked with God was drunk and naked. The tabloids would be willing to pay top dollar for this image of indecency. Ham could not wait to tell his brothers about what he had seen. "There he was, naked as a jay bird. Lying passed out on the floor. I couldn't believe it. He was drunk! What do you guys think?"

This was not Noah's best behavior. We do not know if he intended to get drunk or if he just had one too many. Whatever the case, this was not a moment that Noah was proud of. This is the only record we have of such overindulgence and so it is apparent that this was not Noah's normal way of acting. I am sure that he did not want to be known for this lapse in good judgment, especially in the eyes of his sons. He would have preferred for this chapter of his life not to have been read out loud. Ham was a gossip and, like all good gossips, he told his brothers about their father's condition.

You have no doubt been in similar situations. Maybe you didn't passed out in a bar, but you did something embarrassing. Your good judgment took the night off, and you behaved in a way that is out of character. Your example was awful, and you wish that you could erase it, but you can't. It's out there now and the gossips can't wait to tell anyone who will listen.

I can relate to this story. Like Noah, even preachers at times do something outside of their usual way of acting. A few years ago, I was the talk of the town. An individual was working very hard to destroy my family. So in anger, I hit him. (Something I'm not proud of.) I had made the newspaper many times in the past, usually for services offered to the community or an award that was given in my honor. This time there were no accolades, just a record of my out-of-control behavior and it made the front page. Ham was waiting...

Gossip loves a great story.

People like Ham eagerly anticipate the day someone gives them something to talk about. A drunk, naked preacher (Noah, not me) makes a great story. Trust me, I get it. It is difficult to resist the urge to share something like that. You must admit that as far as gossip goes, this one was a doozy. Your flesh can't wait to spill something so jaw-dropping. Once you know it, keeping it to yourself is not the usual protocol. In our world of texting and instant messaging, news is spread as fast as we can type. Once Ham found out, he instantly messaged his brothers.

Now that Noah's other two sons had been made aware of their father's condition, they are going to teach us a valuable lesson on how gossip should be handled.

"But Shem and Japheth took a garment and laid it across their shoulders; then they walked in backward and covered their father's naked body. Their faces were turned the other way so that they would not see their father naked" (Genesis 9:23, NIV).

These two boys did not cover up what their father had done. Nor were they in denial and pretending that his drunken behavior never happened. They did, however, cover him up. There is a huge difference in those two scenarios. A cover-up and a covering up are not the same. They came in backward with a blanket between them and left without learning the details. The blanket was designed to avoid further disgracing their father. A gossip exposes the nakedness of others and by doing so, rumors are unnecessarily spread. Covering someone to avoid future disgrace is not on a gossip's to-do list.

When Ham found Noah in such a compromising position, he should have found a blanket and covered him up himself. Instead, he left his father naked and disgraced and ran to tell his brothers all about what he had witnessed. If Ham had done the covering himself, his brothers would have discovered their father sleeping comfortably under a blanket in his tent. The entire thing could have been avoided. Remember, I am not suggesting that you aid in covering up someone's indiscretion, only that you cover them up by not spreading the matter. What is not your business is none of your business. The next time someone approaches you with news of Noah's drunken behavior, remember to walk in backward and place the blanket, not share it with the world. Unless their behavior is illegal or puts someone in jeopardy, it is not your duty to be a mandatory reporter. God would prefer that you tuck them in rather than rat them out.

Shem and Japheth went on to become blessed by God. God cannot resist blessing someone with a trustworthy spirit. By keeping the matter concealed, they received God's nod of approval. The blanket they spread over their father became a blanket of blessing spread over them and their future descendants. Ham had a much different fate. He became a slave to his brothers. Gossip makes slaves of us. We become chained to the idea of propagating the rumor. When you live to tell all you know, it won't be long until you have a reputation.

Gossip needs a blabbermouth.

"Gossips can't keep secrets, so never confide in blabbermouths" (Proverbs 20:19, MSG).

Are you the town crier? In ancient cultures, town criers were a common means of communication. The person employed oversaw making private announcements public in the streets and market-places. Maybe you have seen one on television. In medieval England, the town crier would walk around ringing a bell and shouting, "Hear ye, hear ye." The population came from every direction to hear the very important message. Satan still employs town criers to communicate what would have otherwise remained private.

Gossip needs two criers—one to cry out the message, another to cry once the message is out. Do the people around you see you as the bell-ringing, whistle-blowing blabbermouth? Do they know that if they want the latest scoop, your house, not Baskin Robbins, is where they should go? When your pastime is gossip, you will quickly develop a reputation. However, it is not a badge of honor. Being a blabbermouth is not something that most people want on their résumé or tombstone.

It is not always easy to see yourself in this light. The best indicator of this behavior is to examine what you do once potentially embarrassing information finds its way to your ears. Do you wring your hands in the anticipated retelling of the gossip, or do you fold your hands to say a little prayer with no intention of spreading it any further? A blabbermouth can take a situation that would have otherwise been short-lived and turn it into something that is difficult for anyone to outlive. While this may sound harsh, the subject here is of the highest importance. I am not trying to hurt feelings by exposing the poor choice of gossip. I realize that those affected by it can spend years trying to fully recover.

Gossip jumps to conclusions.

It was said that the Athenians of the Apostle Paul's time lived only to tell or hear something new. That's the perfect definition of a professional gossip. They live for the next scandal to break, so that they can break the story. Unfortunately, the story is not the only thing that gets broken. Solomon offers this warning, *"A dishonest man spreads strife, and a whisperer separates close friends"* (Proverbs 16:28, ESV).

Most major cell phone companies have what they call the friends-and-family plan. This plan allows you to get a cheaper rate when you're communicating with those in your close circle. A gossip offers a similar service, only their plan isn't to bring people together and their service is more in line with ripping people apart. Whispers of gossip are often louder than the bullhorn of truth. Before you jump to conclusions, you should always dig for facts.

I remember when one of my close friends approached me and wanted to know why I was spreading rumors about her and her family. I was completely taken back by the allegations. Not only did I not say the things that were supposedly said, but I also actually communicated the opposite. The gossip that she was hearing wasn't even close to the truth, yet it was being presented as the truth. Later, I found out that the gossip came from a former disgruntled staff member who was trying to damage my reputation. When he could not find anything to charge me with, he simply made up his own version of the facts.

Whisperers can't be trusted. The scripture is clear when it comes to gossip, reminding us never to act based upon the words of just one person.

"A single witness shall not suffice against a person for any crime or for any wrong in connection with any offense that he has committed. Only on the evidence of two witnesses or of three witnesses shall a charge be established" (Deuteronomy 19:15, ESV).

Never accept something as the "gospel truth" when it is only coming from one source, especially if that person has been prone to gossip to you in the past. The above verse is a good rule of thumb. Two or three trustworthy people establish a truth, not one blabbermouth with an agenda. We are even told to stay away from such a person.

"Whoever goes about slandering reveals secrets; therefore do not associate with a simple babbler" (Proverbs 20:19, ESV).

Gossip tempts those keeping secrets.

A person of character can keep a secret even if that secret belongs to an enemy. Never use gossip as a form of retaliation. It's tempting, but character doesn't play in the mud even when someone rains on your parade. I can think of several examples from my own life, and I'll share one of those.

Not long after I accepted a pastoral position at a new church, one of the longtime members of the congregation began giving me serious problems. I learned that this was nothing new for this person as he had done it to previous pastors for years.

This person disliked everything about me, despite my effort to build a bridge to him. He insulted my family, the way I dressed, my teaching style, and the list goes on. He also had a spiritual arrogance about him and seemed to think he was holier than everyone else, including me. He left me both exhausted and exasperated. After a few years, I left the church and became the administrator at a counseling office.

One day I received a call from this person. He wanted to come by and chat. I had no idea what the situation entailed and was curious as to why he would want to speak with me given our history. Come to find out, he had been ordered by a judge to seek my counseling services for a very serious offense he had committed. While I can't reveal the offense, let's just say it was reputation-destroying and had been going on during the time of my tenure at the church. No one knew anything about the perverse thing he had been caught doing, not even his family, and he was working hard to keep it that way.

This was my chance to set the record straight! In one blow I could undo all the lies and crush every story of gossip. I could expose the truth and reveal him as the worldly person he was trying to present me as. I could spread the gossip! I knew exactly who I could tell, and she would do my dirty work for me. You know the kind of person I am talking about. Telephone, telegraph, tell her. She was the town crier.

The choice was mine to make, and I am happy to report that the matter is still concealed. This person's family is oblivious to his behavior, and even though his character came to light, last I heard, he is still giving his current pastor as much trouble as he gave me. Containing the gossip had more to do with my character than his. He will answer to God for his behavior, and so will I. Even though he was quick to make up things that weren't true, that did not give me the right to spread things that were true. You can be a fire fighter or a fire lighter. It's your choice. The author of James shares this important truth about the damage that can be done when we choose to gossip.

Gossip is an arsonist.

"Likewise, the tongue is a small part of the body, but it makes great boasts. Consider what a great forest is set on fire by a small spark. The tongue also is a fire, a world of evil among the parts of the body. It corrupts the whole person, sets the whole course of one's life on fire, and is itself set on fire by hell" (James 3:5-6, NIV).

If you want a fire to spread fast, you add an accelerant. Gasoline, for example, amplifies the flames. One drop is all it takes to really get things going. The fastest way to spread hellfire is to spread gossip. Gossip is hell on earth. It's not just the rich and famous of Hollywood who end up getting burnt. Gossip is no respecter of persons and often targets every man or woman. The single mom, the unemployed executive, and the overworked pastor are just a few examples of those who sometimes feel the flames. The fire isn't any less hot when you are unknown.

If the tongue sets the course, where is your tongue taking you? Are your words like kisses from heaven or accusations from hell? Do you burn others down or build them up? The Apostle Paul understood the importance of what we allow to leak from our lips.

"Let no corrupting talk come out of your mouths, but only such as is good for building up, as fits the occasion, that you may give grace to those who hear" (Ephesians 4:29, ESV).

If you must speak about the affairs of others, let it be for the purpose of building rather than demolishing. Corrupt talk is merely the spreading of corruption. It's gossip at its finest. Gossip corrupts our opinions of those we have never met.

It paints a picture of someone based upon the artist's interpretation. It may or may not be an accurate representation of the truth. The Apostle Paul was no stranger to gossip. After his conversion to Christianity, many of the disciples continued to talk about his past. Paul was not always a good man. In fact, at one time he was a very bad man. He had experienced firsthand what it was like to be torn down. It will be difficult for others to become who

God intends for them to be if we are constantly reminding them and everyone else who they used to be. Gracious speech is like the melody of a songbird, pleasant and uplifting. There is nothing gracious about gossip. Gossip has no melody. It's the annoying drone of a mosquito. I will take songbirds over mosquitoes any day!

"With the tongue we praise our Lord and Father, and with it we curse human beings, who have been made in God's likeness. Out of the same mouth come praise and cursing. My brothers and sisters, this should not be. Can both fresh water and salt water flow from the same spring?" (James 3:9-11, NIV).

Gossip is salty.

The above verse is sobering. The same tongue that sings the praises of the Heavenly Father is often used to destroy an earthly brother. James nailed it when he said, "This should not be."

Gossip is salty. Salt water is also dead water. Human consumption leads to dehydration and eventually death. Gossip doesn't drain the life out of us. It drains the life out of the person who has become our target. The salt in our speech makes life for them toxic. Gossip craves salt.

Fresh water, on the other hand, spreads life everywhere it goes. It's nourishing and feeds its environment. Fresh water is the only thing on the planet that is necessary for life to exist. Gossip cannot swim in fresh water. The purity will push it to the bottom and there it will drown. Think about it like this.

"The mouth of a good person is a deep, life-giving well, but the mouth of the wicked is a dark cave of abuse" (Proverbs 10:11, MSG).

When your mouth is a well of life, gossip will not proceed from your lips. Like the gentle rains of spring, your words will cause rapid growth in those around you. The nourishment provided by your speech will create an environment where others can flourish. The only thing gossip grows is chaos. Dreams, reputations, and even families get washed away in the downpour of rumors. Satan would love to partner with you in the storm. He makes himself known in the destruction.

If you have been a gossip in the past, you now have a clear choice to make. Gossip, like any other sin, must first be exposed. Remember, you can't change what you won't acknowledge. While it is easy to dismiss gossip as being a lesser evil than some of the other things God tells us not to partake of, you must remember the consequences are just as extreme. This behavior, in my opinion, is one of the most treacherous. The victims often do not know they are being victimized. Decide to come up higher! Make up your mind that if the devil has something to say, you will not be his mouthpiece. Tell gossip that you're not on the payroll and that if it has something to communicate, your choice is not to be the one doing it.

"*Dear Lord, I am sorry for all times I have spread rumors, talked about my fellow man, destroyed reputations without even having all the facts, and pretended to be concerned when in truth I just wanted to share gossip. Forgive me for being the town crier. I will not use my tongue to spread hellfire. From this day forward, help me to use my mouth as a well of life rather than a cave of abuse. Like the sons of Noah, I will cover those who find themselves in embarrassing situations. Even when something is true, I will not broadcast the matter by being the devil's DJ. From this day forward, I surrender complete control of my tongue to the Lordship of Jesus Christ. I will use my words to build and bless those in my world. I refuse to allow salty speech to kill the hopes, dreams, and futures of those around me. I declare that I am no longer a gossip. In Jesus' name, amen.*"

REFLECTION QUESTIONS

1. Consider the various ways you have been unintentionally making the choice to spread gossip. How will you approach reversing this behavior in the future?

_____

_____

_____

_____

_____

_____

_____

_____

"It takes fuel to have a fire—a fire dies down when you run out of fuel. So quarrels disappear when the gossip ends" (Proverbs 26:20, TPT).

2. Describe how your life has been unfairly affected by those who choose to gossip. Have you committed this to God? Have you forgiven them?

_____

_____

_____

_____

_____

_____

_____

_____

_____

"Bless those who curse you, pray for those who mistreat you" (Luke 6:28, NIV).

3. Identify how you can use your tongue to build up and bless those around you. How will you use your words to impart grace?

_____

_____

_____

_____

_____

_____

_____

_____

_____

"Kind words are like honey—sweet to the soul and healthy for the body" (Proverbs 16:24, NLT).

RELAXED CONVICTIONS

AVOIDING AN AFFAIR

*"One evening David got up from his bed and walked around
on the roof of the palace. From the roof he saw a women bathing.
The woman was very beautiful"*

(2 Samuel 11:2, NIV).

"As so often happens with Washington scandals,
it isn't the original scandal that gets people in the most
trouble—it's the attempted cover-up."

– Tom Petri

What could be more relaxing than a hot bath on a cool spring evening? Bathsheba wasn't the only thing relaxing that night. So were the convictions of a warrior poet. Bathsheba was getting rid of the dirt. David was inviting it. She washed. He watched. The dirt was not thrown out in the bath water, it was thrown in the face of God the Father.

Relaxed convictions give your conscience the night off.

"Prepare for battle!" Joab, the commander of David's army, declared. It was spring and the Ammonites needed to be dealt with. The armies of Israel were on the march. Joab led them out. King David, however, decided to stay home. His decision not to engage the enemy opened a door, a door for David to let down his guard.

David's battle résumé was spotless. He was more than a king. He was also a soldier. However, the devil isn't impressed with heaps of conquered Philistines. He doesn't care that you keep the bloody head of a dead giant in your backpack. He only needs you to take a break from fighting. The devil offers a hiatus. He recommends a break from your normal behavior. Be careful. The break may break you.

There she was, hiding in plain sight, the wife of Uriah. No shower curtain or even a fig leaf to conceal her naked body. Bathsheba was breathtakingly beautiful. At this point, David had no idea of her identity.

"David sent someone to find out about her. The man said, 'She is Bathsheba, the daughter of Eliam and the wife of Uriah the Hittite" (2 Samuel 11:3, NIV).

Now David knows that Bathsheba is a married woman. He also knows the seventh commandment (Exodus 20:14). Adultery was (and still is) strictly forbidden by God. For David to engage in such reckless behavior, he would have to give his convictions the night off. Unlike Joseph, who refused to have sex with Potiphar's wife (Genesis 39:12), David was a willing candidate. Sometimes the enemy presents an offer when we least expect it. Joseph was expecting Potiphar's wife to make a move. She had been pursuing him for quite some time. David was just walking around his property when the offer presented itself. The prophet Samuel may have chosen David that day at Jesse's house (1 Samuel 16:13), but on this night David chose a woman from Uriah's house. The king was wide awake, but his convictions were fast asleep.

"Then David sent messengers to get her. She came to him, and he slept with her" (2 Samuel 11:4, NIV).

"Who is at my door at this hour? I've already washed and am ready for bed," Bathsheba thought. "My lady, the king has requested your presence." Her husband, Uriah, was not at home. He was a soldier in David's army and part of David's personal bodyguard. He was with the troops that Joab led into battle. She had no way of knowing what the king wanted. Perfumed by the rose petals in her bath water, she approached David. "What would my lord the king require of me this night?" she asked. The rest is history.

"The woman conceived and sent word to David, saying, 'I am pregnant' (2 Samuel 11:5, NIV).

Relaxed convictions give birth to disaster.

The baby belonged to David. The fact that Bathsheba had purified herself from her uncleanness (Leviticus 15:19) before sleeping with him was proof enough. Pregnancy by her husband was impossible. David panicked. David learned the hard way that it was not the sinful act itself that caused the most trouble, but the cover-up that follows.

David thought, "Hide it and no one will know." What he failed to realize was, the deeper you bury what you are trying to hide, the more devastating it will be when the secret finally finds a way to surface. Make no mistake; it will find a way. Like water in a teakettle, it will slowly build steam until it is ready to blow the whistle on what you've done.

A disaster was on the verge of erupting. David could have put a plug in the building volcano. He could have owned up to his lapse in good judgement and corrected the entire thing. He chose not to. His relaxed convictions on that spring evening left him anything but relaxed.

While it is often difficult to own up to the ridiculous things that we sometimes do, it is necessary. King David was at a pivotal point. He could have stopped the bleeding. Instead, he chose a different path.

Once engrossed in a cover-up, it is as if our minds begin to think in reverse. Emotion and panic seize our troubled hearts, and we feel a duty to protect and hide our behavior. Fear is now in the driver's seat. The dirt gets swept under the rug, then we sit on the rug denying that we ever made a mess. The school superintendent who received a DWI, the husband who claims he wasn't the one who erased the history on his computer, and the king who secretly had sex with the wife of one of his bodyguards, we are all the same. Adam used fig leaves to cover his backside. We will use whatever we can get our hands on.

The more we try to bury our poor choices, the more devastating the outcome. Like David, you can even be fooled into believing a cover-up is in your best interest. David forgot that confession is often a cure for lasting consequences, and as a result, he was about to sink to his lowest point.

Relaxed convictions hatch deadly plans.

David arranged for Bathsheba's husband to be brought home from the battlefield. When Uriah came before the King, David questioned him about the war and how his fellow soldiers were holding up. He told Uriah to go home to his wife. David even sent him away with a gift (2 Samuel 11:6-8).

Behind the small talk there was a plan. In essence, David tells Uriah to go home and relax. How thoughtful! More than likely the gift was food from David's table. David was setting the mood. He wanted Uriah to enjoy an evening with his wife, Bathsheba. If he were to have sex with her, then David would be off the hook. No one would have to know about the night his convictions took a vacation. Uriah, however, was a man of principle and character. He did something unexpected.

"But Uriah slept at the entrance to the palace with all his master's servants and did not go down to his house" (2 Samuel 11:9, NIV).

It is hard to imagine the discipline it took for Uriah not to go home. A beautiful woman, hot bath, candlelit dinner, and a night of pleasure awaited him. Most men would jump at the chance. Once confronted, he reminds David that the armies of Israel are camped out in the open field, and he wasn't about to go home to eat and drink and sleep with his wife. David's plan had failed.

David continued in his attempted cover-up anyway. Later that night, David invited Uriah over for dinner and drinks. He got him drunk. The alcohol, however, did not persuade Uriah to go home. The next morning, David found him once again asleep outside the royal palace. A drunken Uriah was still more noble than a sober David. This would have been a great time for David to share his indiscretion. He could have sat Uriah down and told him the whole truth. As difficult and humiliating as that would have been, the consequences could have been far less severe at this point. Since David was the king, Uriah really couldn't have done anything about it anyway. It was Uriah's responsibility to protect the royal family, including this baby. Additional heartache and calamity are avoided when we choose honesty. David, as is so often the case with us, pressed on anyway. When one thing fails to conceal our behavior, we usually move on to plan B. We ignore the fact that unraveling stories lead to unraveling lives.

Relaxed convictions have consequences.

The next morning, David wrote a letter to Joab and sent it with Uriah. The message was clear. Place Uriah in the front of the battle where the fighting is fierce and then withdraw from him so that he will be killed (2 Samuel 11:14-15).

For his obedience, Uriah was shot full of arrows. In David's mind, the cover-up was over. He had successfully tied up all the loose ends. After a period of mourning, Bathsheba was brought to David's house and she became his wife. The baby was born a little early, but no one was the wiser.

"But the thing David had done displeased the Lord" (2 Samuel 11:27b, NIV).

Some scandals have what we call whistleblowers. A whistleblower is someone who reveals wrongdoing. I remember in 1988 when Linda Tripp blew the whistle on President Bill Clinton regarding his affair with White House intern Monica Lewinsky. It was front-page news and led to his impeachment by the House of Representatives. President Clinton maintained his innocence until the whistleblower came forward. Once the information was made public, he had no choice but to confess his infidelity. The whistle blew on David as well.

"The Lord sent Nathan to David" (2 Samuel 12:1a, NIV).

Nathan was a prophet and trusted advisor. God sent him to David with a story. The prophet told David a tale about two men. One was very rich and had many sheep and cattle. The other was a poor man who had nothing but one little lamb that he loved. He raised it and it grew up with him and his children. It drank from his cup and even slept in his arms. To him that lamb was like a daughter. One day a traveler came to the rich man, and instead of taking one of his own sheep to prepare a meal for the traveler, he took the lamb of the poor man and prepared it instead.

At this David became furious. He said, "As surely as the Lord lives this man deserves to die!"

"Then Nathan said to David, 'You are the man!'" (2 Samuel 12:7a, NIV).

David's worst fear was staring him in the face. He wasn't afraid of Goliath, but he was afraid of the truth. The buried was resurrected. Nathan knew all the sordid details. The affair, the murder, and the cover-up had not gone unnoticed by the Lord. The tracks he was covering were leading him to the punishment that he rightly deserved. Had he never made those tracks, things could have turned out differently. Nathan had a question.

Why did you do this evil thing? Nathan didn't understand how David could so easily despise the word of the Lord by having Uriah killed and then taking Uriah's wife as his own (2 Samuel 12:9).

The question piques my interest. Nathan doesn't mention what happened between David and Bathsheba on that spring evening. While it was a great sin, Nathan seems to be more focused on David's attempt to cover it up. As far as we know, David made a one-time mistake with Bathsheba, but as for the rest, it was meticulously planned out. The sin would have been easily forgiven, but the cover-up took a huge toll. David prayed, but it was too late to avoid the consequences.

"Then David said to Nathan, 'I have sinned against the Lord'" (2 Samuel 12:13, NIV).

David suffered for his actions. The sword never left his house, and the child born of adultery died. What David did in secret was now being shouted from the rooftops. Ironically, that's where the whole thing started. David buried what he had done, lies watered it, and it grew. The secret was out. We will never know what David's kingdom might have been had he been honest and forthcoming after his mistake.

It is a good thing for David, and for us, that God is merciful. He gave David and Bathsheba another chance and another son. The baby boy was named Solomon. He became Israel's wisest, richest, and most respected king.

Coincidentally, Solomon gives this advice.

"Can a man walk on hot coals without his feet being scorched? So is he who sleeps with another man's wife; no one who touches her will go unpunished" (Proverbs 6:28-29, NIV).

Perhaps Solomon is referring to the consequences that played out within his own family. After David committed adultery and murder, three of his sons died violently and one of them tried to usurp the throne. Solomon's older half-brothers weren't as innocent as Uriah; they were, however, directly impacted by their father's behavior. The fire David scooped into his lap burned up some of his future blessing.

Relaxed convictions emphasize the moment while downplaying the results.

Why would a king with a vast harem and a wife as rare in beauty as Abigail (1 Samuel 25:3) feel the need to have sex with his married neighbor? What David received from Bathsheba could have easily been attained in his own house, from his own wives. The enemy offers a moment of pleasure but delivers a life of regret. You have probably heard someone say, "I lost myself in the moment."

That is fine in most instances. Your high school prom, your wedding day, or the birth of your children would be appropriate times to get lost in your surroundings. The enemy also offers us moments to get lost in, only there is nothing appropriate about the offers. David lost himself by relaxing his convictions. The man who danced before the Ark of the Covenant now danced with disaster. This happens all too frequently to those in the kingdom of God. Our dancing and our sinning are both done at a fever pitch.

It is impossible to pinpoint an exact cause for David's departure from the truth. He was well-versed in the law and knew the penalty his actions would incur. I have a feeling if we could sit with David and ask him why, he would not have a definitive answer. The man after God's own heart allowed human weakness to trump spiritual strength. David, in this instance, is an example of what not to do when we lower our guard and abandon common sense.

Relaxed convictions wound, but Jesus heals.

Guilty as charged and caught red-handed, you don't know exactly why you did it either. The opportunity presented itself, and as calmly as Bathsheba slipped out of her clothes, you slipped out of your moral conscience. Persuasive words and seductive smooth talk tied your noose like it was a five-hundred-dollar silk tie. You slipped it on, cinched it up, and then pulled the lever that would leave you hanging. Your friends and family are equally confused. Like you, they never saw it coming.

Worse yet, you tried to cover it up. Had you fessed up in the beginning and taken your medicine, it would have never gotten this far. You are in shock at the number of casualties. The archers did not miss their mark. Like Uriah, your life is now full of holes. Relaxed convictions have left you anything but relaxed. Panicked and emotionally shipwrecked, you wonder if you will ever recover.

Quiet your heart and listen; Jesus has something to say to you. *"Lift up your heads, because your redemption is drawing near"* (Luke 21:28b, NIV).

Relaxed convictions create spiritual casualties, but a recovered heart sings a psalm. The enemy fears honesty, admittance, and a willful owning up to what we have done. In future chapters, you will see the catastrophic results of refusing to right a sinking ship. David would make right what he had done wrong. In Psalm 51, we are given a glimpse inside the mind and heart of a distraught king. It is a good thing for us that David found pen and parchment on this night. Genuine repentance and remorse dripped as easily as the ink from his quill. David's prayer was long and full of regret.

"Have mercy on me, O God, according to your unfailing love; according to your great compassion blot out my transgressions. Wash away all my iniquity and cleanse me from my sin" (Psalm 51:1-2, NIV).

David piled on the synonyms. He needed mercy, unfailing love, great compassion, and cleansing. The enemy had already taken too much. Complete honesty was required now. David recognized what he had done as sin. There is no record of David praying in repentance the night of the affair. Sin was the last thing on his mind. Maybe, as is often the case with infidelity, he felt like he deserved a night with Bathsheba. It would have been easy to justify and make a case for his actions. After all he was the king and everything in the land, including Bathsheba, was under his jurisdiction. Why not indulge a little? No one would know anyway, except his messengers who brought her to him. Whatever the scenario, he was now very much aware of what he had done.

"I know my transgressions, and my sin is always before me. Against you, you only, have I sinned and done what is evil in your sight" (Psalm 51:3-4, NIV).

Until you own what you have done, the enemy is still very much in control. David came to the realization of his behavior. Unfortunately for David, the consequences of his actions were what created this epiphany. A dead man, a dead baby, and a disappointed preacher were all stops along the way. Until David admitted his transgression, the devastation would build. God has been leading you to this place as well—the place where the light comes on and now you see what others have been trying to tell you all along. The blinders have been removed. Your excuses no longer matter. Like David, you know your transgressions and are ready to experience change.

"Create in me a pure heart, O God, and renew a steadfast spirit within me. Do not cast me from your presence or take your Holy Spirit from me" (Psalm 51:10-11, NIV).

David's spirit had wavered, and his heart felt dirty. The prayer could not have been more sincere and meaningful. The night he pulled Bathsheba close, he pushed away the Holy Spirit. David hungered for the presence of God that had rested upon him when he was just a boy keeping his father's sheep. It is better to be an anointed shepherd than a scheming king. The cover-up brought more than confusion. It also brought God's noticeable disapproval. David, filled with despair and regret over his actions, is by far the greatest example of what can happen when you are ready to fess up the cover-up.

Uriah's blood was something David could not wash off. There wasn't enough soap in the royal palace to turn red hands flesh-colored again. God would have to do it. The innocent also get caught in the crossfire. We make selfish decisions, and others suffer for our actions. There is never a shortage of victims. David never mentions Uriah by name in his prayer. We can see, however, that Uriah was on David's mind.

"Whoever conceals their sins does not prosper, but the one who confesses and renounces them finds mercy" (Proverbs 28:13, NIV).

David found mercy, and so can you. Like David, I bet there are a few casualties. Maybe no one is dead, but they might wish you were. The pain and grief that you have caused are something that you regret and wish you could take back. The parties involved may or may not be open to your remorse. More than likely, your apology will mean nothing to them. I would advise that you issue one anyway. However, your apology to God means everything to Him.

Relaxed convictions may have taken a toll, but repentance can restore your soul.

Are you ready to receive mercy? Are you ready for the situation to be over in your own heart? There is just something about kneeling before God that I find incredibly humbling. The lower I get, the higher He seems. Kneel. You are now in a position of submission. If you understand the gravity of what you have done and you are ready to admit your sin, pray with me.

"Wash away all my iniquity and cleanse me of my sin. Create in me a pure heart, O God."

Soak for a moment. Allow your callused heart to become pliable again. Forsake your excuses and own what you have done. Say it out loud. Don't worry about the tears, let them fall. Now, lift your hands toward heaven and allow your Father to hug you. The weight is lifting, and your joy is returning. The blood on your hands has been washed off in the sea of God's forgetfulness. You are free from your sin. Now, you can finally relax!

REFLECTION QUESTIONS

Avoiding an Affair

1. Refuse to be alone with someone who has expressed sexual interest in you.

"One day, however, no one else was around when he went in to do his work. She came and grabbed him by his cloak, demanding, "Come on, sleep with me!" Joseph tore himself away, but he left his cloak in her hand as he ran from the house (Genesis 39:11-12, NLT).

2. Avoid prolonged eye contact.

"Don't lust for her beauty. Don't let her coy glances seduce you" (Proverbs 6:25, NLT).

3. Keep the penalty in mind. What will this do to your spouse, children, reputation, etc.?

"So it is with the man who sleeps with another man's wife. He who embraces her will not go unpunished" (Proverbs 6:29, NLT).

4. Be emotionally guarded. Be careful who you reveal intimate details of your life to.

"It is better to take refuge in the Lord than to trust in people" (Psalm 118:8, NLT).

5. Foster accountability.

"But they will have to give account to him who is ready to judge the living and the dead" (1 Peter 4:5, NIV).

6. Engage in regular marital sex.

"Your sex life will be blessed as you take joy and pleasure in the wife of your youth" (Proverbs 5:18, TPT).

7. Devote personal prayer time to your marriage. Ask God to place a hedge of protection around you and your spouse.
"You have always put a wall of protection around him and his home and his property" (Job 1:10, NLT).

8. Never entertain sexual fantasies about other people.
"However, I say to you, if you look with lust in your eyes at the body of a woman who is not your wife, you've already committed adultery in your heart" (Matthew 5:28, TPT).

9. Treat all social media and text messages as if your spouse is going to read them.
"Woe to those who go to great depths to hide their plans from the Lord, who do their work in darkness and think, 'Who sees us? Who will know?'" (Isaiah 29:15, NIV)
"What sorrow awaits those who try to hide their plans from the Lord, who do their evil deeds in the dark!" (Isaiah 29:15a, NLT)

10. Speak positively about your spouse and refuse to share negative details about your marriage.
"The tongue can bring death or life; those who love to talk will reap the consequences" (Proverbs 18:21, NLT).

Take a moment to reflect on each of the above scenarios. If you're married, think about how each one applies to your marriage and whether there are things that you need to change. How are you doing? Do you need to make any changes?

_____

_____

_____

_____

_ARROGANCE

YOU CAN'T TELL ME WHAT TO DO

*"Samson went down to Timnah and saw there a young Philistine woman.
When he returned, he said to his father and mother,
'I have seen a Philistine woman in Timnah; now get her for me as my wife'"*

(Judges 14:1-2, NIV).

*"For people who hate discipline and only get more stubborn,
there'll come a day when life tumbles in and they break,
but by then it'll be too late to help them"*

(Proverbs 29:1, MSG).

It was an ordinary day in Zorah, a small village in Dan. Manoah and his wife fed the goats, chased the chickens out of the garden, and prayed to the God of heaven for a son. Like Sarah and Rebekah before her, Manoah's wife needed a miracle if she were to conceive. God had a son in mind, and not just any son. The boy would be a champion of great strength and power. The name Samson would soon cause even the bravest of Philistine warriors to quiver.

The day came when Manoah's wife had a very unexpected visitor. This was no ordinary man. "He looked like an angel and was very awesome," she said. In my mind I picture him tall, chiseled in appearance, with a voice that makes James Earl Jones sound soprano. He had a message for her. It was a message from God.

"The angel of the Lord appeared to her and said, 'You are barren and childless but you are going to become pregnant and give birth to a son" (Judges 13:3, NIV).

The message was direct and to the point. There is a baby boy coming, hide the grape juice! The boy was to be a Nazirite and set apart to God from birth (Judges 13:5). In those days a Nazirite vow was typically voluntary, but in this case, God was firm. This vow consisted of three main obligations. According to Numbers 6, the participant was to:

 *Abstain from all substances that contain any trace of grapes, including intoxicating liquors.

 *Refrain from cutting the hair of one's head.

 *Not become ritually impure by contact with a corpse.

These three requirements were coupled with an obligation to be set apart and holy to the Lord. The Lord made it clear that the vow must be fulfilled according to the law of the Nazirite (Numbers 6:21).

Once the angel departed, Manoah became nervous. He prayed to the Lord that the angel would revisit and teach them how to raise the pint-size deliverer of Israel. God heard Manoah and the angel came back. The message was the same. No grapes, no scissors, and no funeral parlors. His exit was dramatic. While Manoah and his wife offered a burnt offering to the Lord, the angel leaped into the fire and in a flash, he was gone! His words about the boy, however, came true.

Samson's childhood remains a mystery. We know that after his birth, the Lord blessed him, and the spirit of the Lord stirred inside of him (Judges 13:24). We can only image the mischief the boy Samson might have gotten himself into. I can hear the taunts of his friends. "I bet you can't lift that goat over your head." "Oh yeah, I can do it with one hand!" We are not sure of the exact moment Samson realized he was different from the rest.

I have often wondered what Samson looked like. I grew up in the era of Sunday School picture boards. Maybe you remember those. The teacher used felt to attach characters to a biblical scene. I formed my first impression of Samson while looking at the felt cutouts stuck to a board. He always looked like Arnold Schwarzenegger with Angelina Jolie's hair. He looked more like a professional body builder and shampoo salesman than a seafaring Danite. I, however, have never bought into the image of broad shoulders and rippling biceps. Samson's strength came from God. I see him as smaller than most. I also picture his opponents with mouths wide open as God's awesome power was easily put on display. The old prophet Zechariah knew about the kind of power Samson had. It came from God.

"'Not by might nor by power, but by my spirit,' says the Lord Almighty" (Zechariah 4:6b, NIV).

Arrogance demands our strength; humility depends upon God's.

From the very beginning of Samson's adult life, the Bible gives glimpses of his flawed character. If he were an ordinary man, this might have slipped under the radar, but Samson was no ordinary man. Like Samuel after him, Samson was a judge in Israel. Judges were Jewish leaders who arose during a period when there were no ruling kings. Their purpose was to unify the people and deal with spiritual problems. Judges were held in high honor and looked up to as cultural and spiritual examples. A corrupt judge would cause quite a stir, especially one who was spiritually arrogant enough to believe that the law of God did not apply to him.

Like any good judge, Samson knew the law. He was well versed on the topic of intermarriage with heathen nations as outlined in Deuteronomy 7.

"Do not intermarry with them. Do not give your daughters to their sons or take their daughters for your sons, for they will turn your children away from following me to serve other gods" (Deuteronomy 7:3-4, NIV).

I need to point out that mixed marriage has nothing to do with the color of our skin and everything to do with the condition of our hearts. A mixed marriage, from God's point of view, consists of light and darkness. God prohibited marriage with the pagan people of Canaan, and for good reason. Samson ignored the very laws he was born to uphold. It is hard for me to grasp Samson's thought process. Perhaps it was his great strength or even his position as judge that made him feel entitled. Something was whispering, "You are above the commands of God." Spiritual arrogance comes with a price.

Arrogance doesn't follow God's commands.

After a visit to Timnah, Samson was smitten by a young Philistine woman living there. Once he returned home, he requested his parents arrange for them to be married (Judges 14:1-2).

Samson's parents certainly didn't share in his enthusiasm. The angel who had visited them twice was very specific about how Samson was to be brought up and how he was to live as an adult. They were reluctant to bring home a bride who was not bound by covenant to the Lord. This would be front page news at the *Zorah*

Times. "Extra, extra read all about it! Nazirite judge marries a forbidden Philistine."

The pride of Zorah, the luxurious locks of Dan, and his departure from the Law of Moses were no doubt the talk of the town. As with all bad choices, Samson's marriage to the Philistine woman did not go as planned and eventually ignited a firestorm. The result was catastrophic for the Philistines. Samson went ballistic.

He caught three hundred foxes and tied them together tail to tail in pairs. He then fastened a torch to every pair, lit the torches, and let the foxes loose in the standing grain belonging to the Philistines (Judges 15:4-5).

The situation in Timnah was the first of many bad experiences involving women. Before Samson was caught up in the burning of the Philistine grain fields, he was caught up in his own arrogance. Like Adam, Samson's weakness for forbidden fruit proved fatal. This story, as is always the case, started innocently enough, but quickly began to spiral out of control.

Reluctantly Samson's parents gave in to his demand for a Philistine wife. The title of this book perfectly sums up their behavior. They were good people who made a very bad choice. As they approached the vineyards located just outside the city, something unexpected happened. A lion came roaring out at them! Spiritual arrogance always lets the lion loose. Arrogance rings the dinner bell. Mouthwatering, stomach growling, the lion stalks those who believe God somehow excluded them when He was communicating the principles of His word. Today would be a rare treat, the lion would taste Israelite flesh. Or would he?

"The Spirit of the Lord came upon him in power so that he tore the lion apart with his bare hands" (Judges 14:6a, NIV).

Arrogance is a devouring lion.

The lion was dead, but not done with Samson. It was a setup. Sometimes the enemy will allow you to win small battles if it means that you will eventually lose the war. The encounter with the lion only fed Samson's ego. The quest continued. Samson did not mention the lion to his parents. Upon arrival, he met the young Philistine woman. She was his type, exotic and nothing like the Hebrew woman his parents had in mind for him.

Later, Samson returned and the marriage took place. On his way back to Timnah, Samson stumbled across the remains of the dead lion. To his surprise, a swarm of bees had made it their home and the carcass was full of honey. Samson, in arrogance, forgot his Nazirite vow, reached inside the unclean cavity of the lion, and scooped out a handful of the delicious honey. Samson knew better, but he didn't do better. Is that a picture of your life? You know that you shouldn't, but the honey looks so appetizing that you justify your actions? In arrogance you believe you are above the consequences?

During the wedding feast, Samson did the predictable. He made a game out of his departure from covenant. Arrogance never takes covenant seriously.

"Let me tell you a riddle," Samson said to them. "If you can give me the answer within seven days of the feast, I will give you thirty linen garments and thirty sets of clothes. If you can't tell me the answer, you must give me thirty garments and thirty sets of clothes."

"Tell us the riddle," they said. "Let's hear it."

He replied, "Out of the eater, something to eat; out of the strong something sweet." (Judges 14:12-14, NIV)

This, of course, was a depiction of the lion carcass filled with honey. When the Philistines could not answer the riddle, they began to threaten Samson's new wife with the death of her entire family. She threw herself at Samson and through tears pressed him until he told her the answer. She, in turn, gave the explanation to her people. The bet was lost.

In a fury, Samson went to Ashkelon, stuck down thirty of their men, stripped them of their belongings, and gave their clothes to those who had explained the riddle. Leaving his wife in Timnah, Samson returned home. Since he'd abandoned her, she was given to a friend who had attended the wedding. In all likelihood, it was one of his thirty companions. Later, when Sampson returned to get her, he was informed of the exchange. Samson was furious. He burned their grain fields, olive groves, and vineyards. Once the Philistines realized that Samson was exacting revenge over his wife being given to another man, they burned both her and her father to death.

Arrogance creates casualties.

In Samson's first brush with his own ego, we find death, destruction, and deliberate disobedience. The casualties were massive. Samson knew what the Lord required of him, but in arrogance he took a nonchalant approach to obedience. It came with a high price and still does. This would have been a good time for Samson to reevaluate and think about his covenant with God. The Philistine woman and the dead carcass were both forbidden, and both cost him dearly. Once engrossed in spiritual arrogance, it is easy to forget that compromise leads us down a trail of heartache. The end result did not have to be this catastrophic. Tragedy is for those who refuse to learn from their failures. We forget that we can stop at any time and come to Jesus, allowing him to pour His grace upon our disgrace.

Samson, however, did not stop. He continued to viciously slaughter the Philistines. Since they were dumb enough to repay the burning of their crops with the death of the woman he loved, he kept attacking. He killed one thousand of them with the fresh jawbone of a donkey. Samson judged Israel for twenty years. His administration was marred with out-of-control behavior. He just never learned.

In the United States, political scandals are often referred to by adding the suffix "gate." No doubt the most famous example of this is the documents stolen from the Watergate complex during the Nixon administration. Samson's next act of arrogance also involved a gate.

"One day Samson went to Gaza, where he saw a prostitute. He went in to spend the night with her" (Judges 16:1, NIV).

Gaza was an important Philistine seaport on the Mediterranean coast just southwest of Canaan. We are not told of the purpose for this visit. We only know that, upon arrival, something or, better yet, someone caught his eye. While Samson certainly possessed physical strength, he lacked moral strength. Once again, in arrogance, he ignored the laws of his fathers and did the detestable.

Arrogance loves to travel.

In this story, I picture Samson as a businessman. He is in a strange city away from the familiar sights and sounds of home. However, he is not by himself, a lion circles nearby. The lion licks his chops at another opportunity to bring down Israel's champion. While prostitution was not illegal in Gaza, it was immoral, especially for an Israelite judge. But even if he weren't a judge, he was still commissioned by God and given requirements as a Nazarite. Samson willfully ignored the Lord again. Solomon spoke of the dangers of prostitution.

"For an adulterous woman is a deep pit and a wayward wife is a narrow well. Like a bandit she lies in wait and multiplies the unfaithful among men" (Proverbs 23:27-28, NIV).

In every culture, ancient and current, there is no shortage of scenarios involving prostitutes. From high-ranking government officials to well-respected members of the clergy, this story is all too frequent. Samson was both. The bait for this trap is not a squiggly worm on a hook, nor is it easily rejected. The bait is fragrant, soft, and promises pleasure. Like many Old Testament cities, the place where Samson lay was guarded with thick walls and a gate. His heart, however, was left unguarded.

Arrogance needs you to let down your guard.

Once the men of the city were made aware of Samson's location, a plan was formed. They would wait until dawn and kill him. Samson did the unexpected. He got up in the middle of the night, took hold of the city gate, and together with the post tore them loose. He lifted them to his shoulders and carried them to the top of the hill. His strength was still with him, but then again, so was God. For the moment.

Samson's last departure from covenant is his most famous and led to his ultimate demise. Locks of Love had an entirely different meaning in this encounter. Her name was Delilah.

Samson gave the explanation of the riddle to his Philistine wife. He gave his morality to the Philistine prostitute. To Delilah, he gave his life. The lion was circling again. This time Samson would not kill it. One final pounce and all would be lost.

Delilah was an opportunity. While she wasn't a good match for Samson, she was a great match for his moral collapse. After twenty years of trying, the enemy finally found the right partner. Once Delilah's relationship with Samson was made public, the Philistine rulers approached her, and a deal was struck. Eleven hundred shekels of silver from each of the Philistine lords, roughly the price of 275 slaves, was her reward for finding out the secret of his great strength.

I see her, batting her eyelashes, one hand on his shoulder, and the other stroking the hair he knew he had to protect.

"Do you love me, baby?" she says seductively.

"You know I love you," he replies.

"Tell me then, my love, why are you so strong?"

Samson loves her, but he doesn't trust her. In desperation to keep the real source of his power concealed, he begins telling her a series of lies. I've been spending some extra time at the gym. It's this new supplement. I'm getting extra sleep these days. All lies! Those of course were not the actual made-up statements that he used to appease her, but you get the point. She wanted to know and pressed him until he spilled the beans.

"If you tie me up with seven fresh bow strings, I will be as weak as any other man."

He snapped the bow strings like twigs.

"If you secure me with new rope, I will be as weak as a kitten."

He destroyed the rope like it was nothing more than a paper chain.

Is it just me or should Samson have realized by now that this woman was trouble? Delilah was relentless and determined to make him weak. It was obvious. Spiritual arrogance says, "I am trouble, but I am also worth your while. Now, go back to sleep."

Samson continues, "If you weave my hair into a loom, that will do it for sure."

Samson wakes up with his hair firmly wrapped in the rollers of the loom. The loom exploded into splinters once he realized what was happening.

Arrogance takes you one step closer to destruction every time you ignore a red flag.

I am not sure if Samson was in denial or just overly infatuated with Delilah. One thing is for sure—there were plenty of red flags. Every time he told her what to do in order to take his strength, he woke up in that very predicament. There were red flags in every direction. God uses red flags to get our attention and make us aware of immediate danger. Like the warning light on our car engines, red flags warn us that something is not right. The Holy Spirit desperately tries to flag us down before we drive off the cliff. Samson, in his arrogance, paid no attention to the obvious signs all around him. Delilah, after all the failed attempts to rob Samson of his strength, eventually accused Samson of making a fool of her. Finally, he revealed the true source of his power and in arrogance, he found out real fast that he was the fool. Arrogance says, "Consequences, what consequences?"

He told her everything. "I am a Nazirite set apart for God's service and no razor has ever been used on my head. If my head were shaved, my strength would vanish, and I would become as weak as an ordinary man" (Judges 16:17).

With his head in her lap and her knife in his back, Samson fell asleep. The tent flap opened, and in walked the lion—the destroyer. The enemy of everything God had formed Samson to become was now standing close enough to strip him of the future. The seven braids of his hair fell to the dirt floor, taking his strength with them. The Philistines burst onto the scene and Samson awoke. "Don't worry, babe. I got this," he said.

Next, came what is possibly the saddest verse in the Bible.

"But he did not know that the Lord had left him" (Judges 16:20b, NIV).

Samson betrayed his calling and permitted another Philistine woman to rob him of his special consecration to the Lord. The Lord's champion was now helpless to defend himself from his captors. He was seized, his eyes were gouged out, and he was, ironically enough, taken to Gaza, the very place he spent the night wrapped in the arms of a prostitute. The lion offered no honey this time, only imprisonment.

Blind and robbed of his mane, the pride of Zorah was reduced to grinding grain in a Philistine jail.

Arrogance is heartless, taking your reputation and legacy.

I'm sure it didn't take long for the news of Samson's shame to reach Israel. Manoah and his wife were powerless to help their son. The legendary muscleman and killer of a thousand was brought low by the glances of a single woman.

Samson had plenty of time to think about his actions while in prison. The millstone was heavy, but his heart was heavier. I can see him palming the top of his head. "What have I done? How could I have been so foolish as to believe that I could disobey the Lord and not pay for it?" he thought. He lost more than his seven braids. He also lost God's presence. The absent weight of his hair was nothing compared to the absent weight of God's spirit. He was alone, and the biggest agony he faced was the knowledge that he had done it to himself through his arrogant disobedience. Samson felt entitled, like the rules didn't apply to him. They did. Spiritual pedigrees, works, and religious duties carry little weight in heaven's courtroom. Even a judge's robe can become like filthy rags.

Redemption cries out, "Samson, it's a new day!"

"But the hair on his head began to grow again after it has been shaved" (Judges 16:22, NIV).

Before the spirit of God returned to Samson, he was publicly disgraced, spiritually bankrupt, and privately humiliated. Samson was so low he would have to look up to tie his shoes. I have to believe that it was more than just his hair that began to grow back. Perhaps his mind drifted to the stories his father had told him about the day an awesome-looking angel came to announce his birth. His destiny had taken a wrong turn, and he knew it.

This story ended in a grand finale, like the final explosion at a Fourth of July fireworks display. The Philistines assembled to offer a sacrifice to Dagon, their god. Samson was the entertainment. After all, his defeat was a huge prize. This man married and abandoned one of their women, obliterated their fields, and humiliated their army by defeating them with a donkey's jawbone. But they showed him. They were the better men. They defeated him by using his weakness against him. Now they would humiliate him and his God by putting him on display at a service to their heathen god.

Once inside the temple filled with three thousand Philistines, Samson asked the servant leading him to position his hands on the support pillars that held the temple. There, surrounded by enemies,

Samson prayed his final prayer.

"Then Samson prayed to the Lord, 'Sovereign Lord, remember me. Please, God, strengthen me just once more, and let me with one blow get revenge on the Philistines for my two eyes" (Judges 16:28, NIV).

Samson pushed, and the temple fell. He too would die that day, having killed more Philistines—the enemies of God—in his death than in his life. Samson found God, or better yet, God found Samson. His strength returned to the kid from Zorah. The Holy Spirit, once driven away, was back and on full display.

The story of Samson serves as a warning to those who push the Spirit of God aside, believing there will be no fallout. When we forget our covenant vows, we can only expect dire consequences. Samson recovered his strength, but only after he hit bottom.

Arrogance takes us to the bottom, but we don't have to stay there.

Perhaps you can relate. You wake up in a self-imposed prison. You begin the daily grind only to realize that tomorrow will be exactly the same as today. Your lover and your dignity are both gone. "What have I done?" echoes through your shaved head. The locks of your hair lay piled in the corner of a rundown apartment, reminding you of what you gave up before everything blew up. You are at your lowest point. Without hope, you fall to your knees and put your hands on your head. Wait, it can't be! It's growing back!

Spiritual recovery usually begins at the bottom. Like Samson, God is not finished with you. What you have allowed Delilah to cut away can be restored. Your covenant with God does not have to remain severed. Your behavior has not taken you past the limit of God's grace, nor have you exhausted the scope of His mercy. Even if, like Samson, you have arrogantly repeated the same immoral behavior over and over again, all is not lost. You can bounce higher than you fell. Arrogance does not have to win. Samson's prayer was brief and honest.

"O Lord, remember me and strengthen me," Samson said. There is a noticeable absence of excuses in this prayer and not even a mention of Delilah. This could not be pinned on his parents, the prostitute, or even the persistence of a Philistine beauty. This was Samson's fault, and he was ready to own it. He wanted to be forgiven, remembered, and strengthened. God had not forgotten Samson. He watched as he sank deeper and deeper into the cesspool of disobedience. God seldom interrupts us while we are sinning. He silently whispers to our hearts, "Come back." God waited patiently and listened lovingly for Samson's prayer. God smiled the day Samson prayed. God has been saving a smile for you as well.

If you have broken your covenant with God and forgotten the true source of your strength, it is quite probable that you feel as if you've forfeited your future. Ego has stolen your identity and turned the one-time champ into a chump. Samson's life teaches us that when spiritual arrogance becomes meekness, destiny and purpose are not lost.

Samson was born to kill Philistines (Judges 14:4). After he repented and approached God with a broken and humble heart, he was strengthened, allowing him to kill more Philistines in his death than in his life. Your purpose is waiting on your heartfelt repentance. Your destiny is not yet lost.

Like the servant boy in this story, I have led you to the pillars of the temple. You can feel the smooth marble on your fingertips and hear the insults of the crowd above you. Arrogance brought you here. Now, you decide how it ends. Will the enemy continue to make sport of you, or will you pray and push? With one blow you can change the ending.

Samson could have gone out in a fit of rage. Instead, he went out in a blaze of glory. While he could not take back the disappointment of his parents, the failed marriage, or his moral collapse, he could return to the arms of his Heavenly Father. Samson found his way back, and so can you. Later, we find him mentioned in the Hall of Faith (Hebrews 11:32).

Arrogance doesn't have to end in the Hall of Shame.

There you sit, head down, tears dripping. So much has happened. It would be easier to put toothpaste back in the tube than to undo what you have done. Are you ready for it to be over? Are you ready to begin rebuilding your life, only this time you will apply God's word? If so, pray with me.

"O sovereign Lord, remember me. O God, please strengthen me."

Now, breathe deep. Wait, don't rush! Breathe again. Do you feel that? It's your strength returning. Let it wash over you. Close your eyes and drink deep.

"If we confess our sins, he is faithful and just and will forgive us our sins and purify us from all unrighteousness" (1 John 1:9, NIV).

From Samson, we learn that when spiritual laws are ignored, the consequences can feel like prison. Samson was somehow under the delusion that God had excluded him from right behavior because of his high calling. Simply put, he became too big for his britches. The result was catastrophic. He had more charisma than character. His arrogance took a toll, but like you, he prayed and pushed. Even though it cost him his life, Samson was given another opportunity. God, in his mercy, has given you another opportunity as well. Your hair is growing back. You can braid, blow dry, pin up, or even perm it, if you wish. Never, ever cut it again.

REFLECTION QUESTIONS

1. In what areas of your life are you most tempted to rely more upon what you can do, rather than upon what only God can do?

_____

_____

_____

_____

_____

_____

_____

_____

"Trust in the Lord with all your heart, and do not lean on your own understanding" (Proverbs 3:5, ESV).

2. Do you sometimes justify your wrong behavior? Where are you most likely to make excuses for yourself?

_____

_____

_____

_____

_____

_____

_____

_____

_____

"But they all alike began to make excuses" (Luke 14:18a, ESV).

3. Like the warning light on the dashboard of a car, the Holy Spirit will often wave a red flag anytime something is about to break down in your life. Do you have red flags?

_____

_____

_____

_____

_____

_____

_____

_____

"Likewise the Spirit helps us in our weakness" (Romans 8:26a, ESV).

PRIDE

YOUR WAY IS NOT YAHWEH

*"Your heart became proud on account of your beauty,
and you corrupted your wisdom because of your splendor.
So I threw you to the earth"*

(Ezekiel 28:17a, NIV).

"God sends no one away empty except those
who are full of themselves."

– Dwight L. Moody

Lucifer shimmered as he paced back and forth on streets of gold. The light of the holy city reflected off the jewels adorning his garment with the combined magnificence of every sunset from the creation of time until now. His private thoughts were now made public. The living rainbow presented his case. "Follow me. I could be God," Lucifer campaigned.

Pride wants power, but for the wrong reasons. Pride gave Lucifer a high opinion of himself. He was bursting with self-importance. He may have been the guardian cherub, but he was still no god.

Pride wants you to think you are God.

Lucifer is proof that even when conditions are as amazing as heaven, we are still susceptible to making terrible choices. Pride seldom visits the pig pen. It prefers the comfort of a penthouse suite. Pride needs caviar, not corncobs. Pride sleeps best on silk sheets. Pride forgets that your way is not Yahweh.

This chapter begins with heaven's first supermodel.

*"You were a **model** of perfection, full of wisdom and perfect in beauty"* (Ezekiel 28:12b, NCB).

The 1980s are often referred to as the decade of the supermodel. Raging beauties like Cindy Crawford and Elle Macpherson graced catwalks worldwide. I should know. I was a teenage boy during that era. Supermodels leave an impression.

Heaven had its own version. Lucifer was center stage. It's hard to imagine the magnitude of Lucifer's exquisiteness. The sheer depth of his beauty is unfathomable. With the class of an aristocrat and the charm of Paris at twilight, he stood out from the other angels. Even the archangels, Michael and Gabriel, were not like Lucifer. He was in a class all by himself.

The prophet Ezekiel gives us a glimpse. Decked out in diamonds, this cherub was created blameless. Along with his beauty, Lucifer had one unique asset. He had timbrels and pipes on the inside of him (Ezekiel 28:13-15, KJV). Lucifer didn't play an instrument. He was one. He literally had an orchestra in his throat. His singing probably sounded like the Philharmonic. I am quite sure heaven's peacock did a lot of strutting. He learned the hard way that pride pats your back and trips your feet. It puffs you up and pulls you down.

"He may become puffed up with conceit and fall into the condemnation of the devil" (1 Timothy 3:6b, ESV).

While God does want all his creation, both earthly and heavenly, to have self-esteem and consider their lives valuable, He also demands complete dependency and allegiance. Lucifer went rogue. His success and exceptional musical gifts were something to be proud of, but instead of using them to reflect God's glory, he committed high treason and sought to reflect his own.

I pose several questions regarding pride. How do we see ourselves as kings and priest (Revelation 5:10) without becoming haughty and arrogant? How do we celebrate our success without celebrating ourselves? How can we be proud of who we are and our accomplishments without being filled with pride? Lucifer is an example of how destructive pride can be.

Pride builds you up and then burns you down.

As I write this chapter, I can hear the sirens of a fire truck just outside my office window. As a boy, I loved fire engines. The shiny red and chrome always generated excitement and got my full attention. Like most young boys, I wanted to be a fireman when I grew up. Now that I am a man, the sirens make me cringe. Something is burning. What was, no longer is.

"How you have fallen from heaven, morning star, son of the dawn!" (Isaiah 14:12, NIV).

Lucifer's pride spilled out, and heaven was never the same. Heaven's worship leader wanted to be the pastor. He wasn't qualified and, worse yet, he was building his own congregation. Pride turns us into troublemakers and archangels into devils. No wonder the Lord hates it (Proverbs 6:16). Lucifer fell hard.

Ironically, the person enveloped in pride is usually the last to know. Others sometimes see it. Those under pride's grip usually don't. They feel as if they are different from the rest. It's not their fault their ideas are superior. They are just ahead of the game, or so they think. The angel of light was in the dark about his personality flaw. That is the only way we can account for his rebellion. Pride is cunning. It speaks our language. It tells us exactly what we want to hear.

"For if anyone thinks he is something, when he is nothing, he deceives himself" (Galatians 6:3, ESV).

The only thing worse than deception is self-deception. Despite opposing evidence and the logical argument that he could in no way replace God, Lucifer marched forward without regard for the obvious outcome. For pride to succeed, it must first deceive you. Once deception is deeply rooted in your own mind, then trouble comes.

Pride doesn't listen.

Like a member of Satan's Special Forces, pride silently creeps into your life and establishes a secure perimeter. You become base camp. Arrogance, conceit, and self-importance are established as boundary lines around your heart. The domineering husband, the sister who believes she knows more than her siblings, the pastor who thinks he is God's gift to the world, and the archangel who can't stop staring in the mirror at his own reflection are all the same— pride-soaked and heaven-rejected.

Pride doesn't listen. Why should it? Pride knows more than anyone in the room, including God. Pride invites you to dinner, announces how magnificent it is, and lets you pick up the check. Pride needs followers, and so did Lucifer.

Lucifer convinced one-third of heaven's population to follow him into rebellion. As a result, war broke out. Lucifer and those who joined him in his efforts to overthrow the Heavenly Father were cast down to the earth (Revelation 12:7-9). Lucifer and his army of "yes" men learned the hard way that lofty opinions of self-importance are no match for the creator of the universe. Easily swatted, like dead flies they were tossed to the ground.

"Pride goes before destruction, and a haughty spirit before a fall" (Proverbs 16:18, ESV).

Pride lies.

Lucifer, like so many, started reading his own fan mail. His haughtiness was no longer hidden. Pride cost him. He not only lost his home, but he also lost his job.

Pride promises you more while covertly taking what you already have. Lucifer went from walking among the fiery stones on the mountain of God to slithering on his belly in the Garden of Eden. He is a prime example of what can happen to an individual when pride distorts their reality. He believed the lie.

Lucifer's arrogance started when he began telling himself things that were not true. Do you talk to yourself? Of course you do! While most people use healthy self-talk to remember daily tasks or as motivation, Lucifer talked to himself about himself.

> *You said in your heart, "I will ascend to the heavens; I will raise my throne above the stars of God; I will sit enthroned on the mount of the assembly, on the utmost heights of the sacred mountain. I will ascend above the tops of the clouds; I will make myself like the Most High"* (Isaiah 14:13-14, NIV).

There is a common thread in the above verses. Did you catch it? Five times Lucifer declares, "I will." Without "I" pride has no power. The Apostle Paul said, "It is no longer I who live, but Christ" (Galatians 2:20, NIV). Lucifer essentially said, "It is no longer Christ, but I." In his heart, Lucifer was setting himself up for failure.

Lucifer was as deranged as he was splendid. His wisdom was clouded by self-importance. The pride he should have swallowed, he vomited onto others. The entire thing could have been avoided if Lucifer had only questioned his motives. Pride convinces us that we can fly, then drives us to the edge of the cliff and watches as we plummet.

Pride promises more but always leaves you with less.

Lucifer's quest to be on top put him at the bottom. Not only did he not gain anything, but he also lost what he already had. Unfortunately, he couldn't see what pride was doing to him and still doesn't. As is the case with so many, pride will not allow you to admit when you have lost. I am quite sure that in Lucifer's mind, he didn't lose. In fact, he believes that one day he will win. Pride is distorted. The facts get lost.

Solomon said it best. *"When pride comes, then comes disgrace"* (Proverbs 11:2, NIV).

Wings clipped, Lucifer and his cohorts crashed to the earth in a fiery blaze. It has always been my opinion that the meteor hitting the earth and destroying the dinosaurs was actually Lucifer being cast from heaven. I picture an enraged angel, stripped of his rank, full of toxic venom, and in the mood for destruction. With all that he had suffered and lost; he would be capable of annihilating an entire planet. Whatever the case, what started out as pride ended in his destruction. Lucifer's high opinion of himself is what brought him low.

Pride pushes for more. More control, more being right, more holding on to grudges, more power, and more recognition. Pride convinces you that more is never enough. This creates a serious problem. When you take more for yourself, you leave others feeling like less. For example, sometimes in marriage one partner is always asserting dominance and seeking control. Like Lucifer, in their mind they believe that this will give them an upper hand and they will have more. What usually happens is the other person involved gets tired of feeling diminished and eventually leaves. So instead of more, they find themselves with less.

This story does not end in repentance or even regret. Pride makes devils of us. Lucifer could not be saved, but maybe you can be. Jesus saw Satan fall like lightning from heaven (Luke 10:18). Maybe He can see you rise. Pride doesn't budge on its own. It fought hard to gain access to your heart. The only way to remove pride is to replace it.

Pride fears humility.

If one-third of the angels fell with Lucifer, then two-thirds refused him. We can only imagine their objection. I am convinced that they were as passionate about serving God as Lucifer was about overthrowing Him. Lucifer apparently could not be convinced, but perhaps I can convince you. Pride fears humility. It is the one thing that can usurp its authority over a heart that has been swooned by its false promises. Pride lets go when humility takes hold.

Humility is often misunderstood. We see humility as weakness and a lack of backbone. That, however, could not be further from the truth. Humility is not thinking less of yourself; it's thinking of yourself less.

This was something Lucifer could not do. For pride to survive, you have to be front and center. The focus of attention must be pointed in your direction. Humility is having a correct view of yourself, the people in your world, and God. Lucifer taught us that when our view becomes obstructed, it creates all kinds of negative consequences.

Pride puts you first. Sometimes, like Lucifer, we are fully aware of our actions and our attempt to be viewed as more important than the people in our world. However, it is more likely that pride has slithered in unnoticed by you.

Perhaps you are reading this chapter and for the first time you realize that others are not the problem. You are the problem. For years you have pinned blame, made excuses for your behavior, and tried to build your own following. Your reckless attempt to always be right, get your way, and diminish the opinions of those around you has left a wake of destruction and broken relationships. The people in your life, including family, are constantly rotating in and out. You have talked yourself into believing that they can't handle your personality. The truth, however, is you can only be tolerated in small doses and others can only handle you for so long.

It's too late for Lucifer, but it's not too late for you. Pride may have barred the door, but humility knocks. Will you open the door? Consider the following lessons on humility and pride that Lucifer never learned:

1. Pride is not a personality trait. Pride is sin.

"But he gives more grace. Therefore it says, 'God opposes the proud but gives grace to the humble" (James 4:6, ESV).

Any behavior that causes God to oppose you can be classified as sin. Pride is not who you are, it's who you have become as a result of sin silently slipping into your heart. Lucifer obviously started off strong, but the pride that infiltrated his heart made him weak. He didn't begin as Satan, Father of Lies. He began as Lucifer, son of the morning. However, his wisdom was corrupted by his splendor. He obviously had past credibility in heaven. Otherwise, he would have been immediately rejected by those who chose to follow him into rebellion. Pride is on a mission to rob you of your identity. Humility is on a mission as well.

However, unlike pride, humility wants to establish your identity in Christ.

Pride acts like any other sin. It looks for a potential host, attaches a few seed thoughts, and waits for the harvest. In my experience, pride typically has more leverage to operate in those with choleric or type A personalities. Lions prowl, sheep follow. Keep in mind this is not always the case. However, pride usually targets the strong and self-confident. Lucifer is a prime example. He was a lion and still is.

As an admitted control freak and full-blown choleric personality type, I will admit that pride has tapped my shoulder more than once. Pride reminds me of everything that I have accomplished, but somehow forgets to mention that I could not have accomplished much without help. Pride gives a PowerPoint presentation of my achievements and right decisions but forgets all my failures and wrong choices. Pride would love to take over and take away everything that I have worked so hard to accomplish. It needs me to believe the same lie that Lucifer believed. *"I will make myself like the Most High"* (Isaiah 14:14b, NIV).

The Apostle Paul hit the nail on the head when he listed pride as one of the works of our flesh (Galatians 5:20). Pride falls into the same class as adultery and idolatry. Pride is a sin. The Psalmist David knew it. He said, *"My heart is not lifted up, my eyes are not raised too high"* (Psalm 131:1, RSV). Lucifer did not accept his over-inflated ego as being sin, and he was brought down to the depths of the pit (Isaiah 14:15). David was lifted; Lucifer was brought down. Humility lifts us up. Pride takes us down. The first step to defeating pride is to see it for what it is—sin.

2. Humility is allowing God to raise you higher.

When you exalt yourself, God will humble you. That is called humiliation.

When you humble yourself, God will exalt you. That is called promotion.

"Whoever exalts himself will be humbled, and whoever humbles himself will be exalted" (Matthew 23:12, ESV).

Lucifer was not about to wait and see if God was interested

in retiring. Pride did what it always does. Pride takes what it wants by force. However, it usually doesn't keep it for very long. What can be gained in a short amount of time can be lost in the same amount of time. This stands in complete contradiction to the kind of humility that Jesus demonstrated at the cross. Gods don't die and wait for resurrection. Jesus did. Jesus demonstrated true humility as He hung suspended between heaven and earth. Even though He had the power to exalt himself and come down off the cross, He chose to die for our sins and trust his Father to exalt Him at the proper time. Jesus waited to be promoted.

Humility waits three days and shows up in new Easter clothes. Pride refuses to wait and leaves you stripped naked. Self-exaltation and self-promotion are symptoms of a heart that is under the sway of pride's strong grip. When you catch yourself forcing and manipulating the situation to get what you want, rather than demonstrating right behavior and waiting for it, that's pride.

3. Pride refuses to decrease.

"He must increase, but I must decrease" (John 3:30, ESV).

Decrease? Certainly not Lucifer, not now, and not ever! Why would heaven's star performer agree to something as ridiculous as that? Truth be told, Lucifer would rather die than decrease. Pride is a power player.

What about you? Are you willing to decrease? Are you willing to become less so that others can become more? That is true humility. Jesus demonstrated this for us by taking the form of a servant. He washed feet, cooked breakfast, and hauled up nets full of fish. In humility He performed these acts of service. Pride serves only itself. Like an unreasonable customer in an overpriced restaurant, pride is full of demands. If by some chance pride does lend a helping hand, it will announce its contribution. Pride must be noticed even when serving.

Lucifer and Jesus both came to the earth from heaven. Lucifer fell because of his desire to increase. Jesus was sent because of his willingness to decrease. When we are humble, God sends us like a Valentine to a hurting world. When we are proud, God casts us from his presence. It is easy to distinguish between those who have been cast out and those who have been sent forth.

4. Humility is never accidental; it is always intentional.

"All of you, clothe yourselves with humility toward one another, because, 'God opposes the proud but gives grace to the humble'" (1 Peter 5:5b, NIV).

Humility—clothe yourself with it. Humility is as intentional as putting your pants on in the morning. If you forget, you are not the only one who will notice!

I have always loved the story "The Emperor's New Clothes." In this short tale told by Hans Christian Andersen, two weavers promise an emperor a new suit of clothes that is invisible to the stupid, incompetent, or those unfit for their positions. When the emperor parades himself around his kingdom in his new clothes, no one dares to tell him that he is naked. Eventually, a child cries out, "He is not wearing anything at all!"

Leave it to a child to speak out loud what everyone else is thinking. No one wanted to tell the king he wasn't clothed, and I am sure that no one wants to tell you, either. They watch as you strut your stuff. In your mind, you are a royal fashion show. In their minds, you are naked and need to be avoided. Clothing yourself in humility only happens when you decide to take off the regal robes of pride. Like the emperor who recognized his nakedness, you've heard a voice saying, "You're naked!" Now you have a decision to make. Clothe yourself in humility, seek forgiveness, and pursue change, or continue to assert dominance, dismiss the emotional wellness of others, and stay the same.

Pride drew Lucifer close by providing just the right bait. Self-exaltation would do it. Lucifer was an easy target. Unlike King David, Lucifer wasn't looking at the neighbor's wife; he was looking at himself. He wasn't seeking pleasure; he was seeking a position. This spiritual problem began in Lucifer's heart and if we are to avoid the same moral collapse, we must examine ours.

Pride hardens our hearts. It's as if we can't see what our behavior is doing to those around us. We are blind to how small and diminished we sometimes make people feel. Our ferocious desire to be right, get what we want, and be the center of attention have always been chalked up to who we are rather than who we have become. We see our strong personality as a leadership quality while forgetting that real leaders give up to go up.

"But whoever would be great among you must be your servant" (Mark 10:43, ESV).

It's dawning on you, isn't it? You are looking back, and you can't believe how you have behaved. You have been to the people in your world what Lucifer was to the other angels in heaven. Proud, arrogant, and downright selfish is what you have been. You're the culprit! The problem wasn't the failed relationship or the broken dream. The problem is what you have allowed yourself to become.

The cry of a tender and humble heart is irresistible to God. It is music to His ears. He hears that cry above all else. The collateral damage you have caused will take some time to reverse, and you have some apologizing to do as well. Not just to God, but to the people that your actions have damaged. Lucifer clung to his proud heart. You can surrender yours.

"I will give you a new heart and put a new spirit in you; I will remove from you your heart of stone and give you a heart of

flesh" (Ezekiel 36:26, NIV).

If you are ready to release your pride, God is ready to take it, forgive it, and throw it in the sea of His forgetfulness. God will forget who you used to be, and in time others will, too! Now that you see your pride as sin, attack it with the same intensity that you would any other area of disobedience. Repent and move forward. Pray what Lucifer should have.

"Cleanse me from what I have become. Take my selfish heart and make it useful again. I am sorry for allowing my own pride to become a stumbling block for others. Forgive me, Lord."

REFLECTION QUESTIONS

1. Are there areas of your life where you've stopped being completely dependent upon God? In what ways have you pushed Him out by relying upon yourself?

_____

_____

_____

_____

_____

_____

_____

_____

"For I, the Lord your God, hold your right hand; it is I who say to you, 'Fear not, I am the one who helps you'" (Isaiah 41:13, ESV).

2. Where you do struggle with the need to always be right or have your own way?

_____

_____

_____

_____

_____

_____

_____

_____

_____

_____

"Be free from pride-filled opinions, for they will only harm your cherished unity" (Philippians 2:3, TPT).

3. How can you begin to demonstrate humility to the people in your world?

_____

_____

_____

_____

_____

_____

_____

_____

"With all humility and gentleness, with patience, bearing with one another in love" (Ephesians 4:2, ESV).

REVENGE

THE AVENGER

"Then Joseph said to his brothers, 'Come close to me.'
When they had done so, he said, 'I am your brother Joseph,
the one you sold into Egypt!'"

(Genesis 45:4, NIV)

"Let go of offence. Let go of fear. Let go of revenge.
Don't live angry. Let go now!"

– Joel Osteen

Revenge is everywhere. It looms on the street corner, sings in the church choir, and works on Wall Street. Those who were wrecked wait to retaliate. Some are subtle. Others are blatant. All are fuming. They won't let it go. Somebody must pay the bill on what was done to them. We too often forget the lover of our souls watches, and He wants to handle it. The writer of Romans understood how important it is to allow God to settle the score.

"Beloved, never avenge yourselves, but leave it to the wrath of God, for it is written, 'Vengeance is mine, I will repay, says the Lord" (Romans 12:19, ESV).

God will handle what has unfairly been done to you. You were never assigned to avenge yourself. He is the hero who takes the score back to zero. If you're planning to go after your offender by yourself, dig two graves; you'll need them both. This behavior is difficult to avoid, as there is no shortage of people who live only to make the rest of us miserable. If you are to conquer the need for revenge, it will not be by accident. Before you set your offender straight, first consider allowing God to set you straight.

There is an Avenger. He is not a science fiction action hero. He doesn't fly with a magic hammer or turn green when He gets angry. He is the maker of heaven and earth. Vengeance is His, and to take it for yourself is robbery. In this chapter we are going to take a close look at the life of Joseph. By examining his attitude, you can learn what to do when revenge taps your shoulder.

Revenge retaliates.

Jacob's boy Joseph may have been handpicked by God, but he wasn't very wise in his relationship with his older brothers, even giving his father a bad report about how they were handling their responsibilities (Genesis 37:1-2). Your calling, no matter how great or significant, doesn't automatically make you a people person. Joseph's difficulty with his brothers started early. Apparently, they weren't taking their shepherd duties very seriously, so Joseph complained about them to their father.

Their exasperation with their little brother continued to build. Revenge doesn't always show itself upon the first offense. Often it grows over time and becomes more powerful as the relationship continues to deteriorate. The situation with the flocks was just one of many offenses, and Jacob wasn't helping matters, either. He blatantly favored Joseph over his other eleven boys because Joseph was born to him in his old age. His partiality to Joseph was clearly seen when he had a robe of many colors made for him. It was the kind worn by a king's virgin daughter. Just getting dressed in the morning reminded Joseph's brothers how insulted they were by their father's actions. They began to hate Joseph and could not speak a kind word to him. Revenge was now whispering, "Get even." Their breaking point came when Joseph shared his dream.

"He said to them, 'Listen to this dream I had: We were binding sheaves of grain out in the field when suddenly my sheaf rose and stood upright, while your sheathed gathered around mine and bowed down to it" (Genesis 37:6-7, NIV).

The brothers were furious. Joseph was insinuating that they would all one day bow down before him. This of course would come to pass, but at the time it felt like the misguided foolishness of an insulting little brother. Perhaps Joseph was so entitled by his dad that he assumed they would be happy to bow to him! This story clearly portrays how revenge needs a catalyst, something to set the payback into motion. The well-dressed tattletale was now making himself out to be ruler over his older brothers. In ancient culture, hierarchy among sons was taken very seriously. The birthright belonged to Reuben, the oldest, not Joseph. This was the straw that broke the camel's back.

Be honest. Whose robe makes you want to barf? Who do you find so insulting that you have started putting together a plan to inflict emotional or even physical pain upon them? Do you have a Joseph?

Revenge waits until the opportunity is right.

Revenge always mentions both the plan to get even and the offense. This story is no different. Joseph's brothers had a plan. They were going to kill Joseph and throw him into a deep pit and then tell their father that he was eaten by a wild animal. The offense was the dream (Genesis 37:17-20).

Revenge needs you to remember why you're getting even in the first place. If you forget, you might not follow through on the promise you made to yourself to make them pay for what they did, said, or caused. You are most susceptible to revenge when you are concentrating your thoughts on the events of yesterday. The older brothers were standing in the present, planning to kill their little brother for something he did in the past. As far as revenge is concerned, to look forward is to forget. And it can't forget the past until the wrongs of the past are righted.

The boys knew that their father would never forgive them if they harmed Joseph. So, they concocted a believable lie. Together they told Israel (Jacob) his beloved son was eaten by a wild animal. In truth, they had hidden their despised little brother in a hole. Revenge wants the injury without claiming responsibility. Revenge wipes its fingerprints off the evidence, erases security camera footage, and deletes all email.

Killing without connection is its best recourse. Revenge says, "Keep it on the down low."

Reuben was the oldest and should have been the most offended by Joseph's dream. He, however, realized his responsibility as firstborn was to protect all his brothers. Reuben stepped forward and said, "Don't take his life or shed his blood. Throw him in the hole." Reuben was secretly planning to rescue Joseph and take him back to their father, but the plan didn't work out that way. Joseph's brothers stripped him of his robe and did as Reuben requested (Genesis 37:23-24).

The robe represented the injury. Joseph was wrapped in Jacob's favoritism and his own dreams of supremacy. They unwrapped him. He was no prince. He was just a boy who needed to be taught a lesson, and revenge was ready to teach. Good thing for Joseph revenge is selfish. His brothers decided to go one step further and try to get a little more out of the deal.

"Judah said to his brothers, 'What will we gain if we kill our brother and cover up his blood? Come, let's sell him to the Ishmaelites and not lay our hands on him; after all, he is our brother, our own flesh and blood.' His brothers agreed" (Genesis 37:26-27, NIV).

Make no mistake money, not mercy, was the deciding factor here. Revenge wanted the silver. Every shekel spent was a reminder of how they had gotten even with their little brother. Disrobed and in what must've seemed like a nightmare, Joseph eventually ended up being sold to Potiphar in Egypt. His brothers dipped his robe in goat's blood, took it back to their father, and planned a funeral. Revenge got what it wanted most—an even score.

Jacob was in the dark about what really happened. As far as he knew, his other sons were in as much pain as he was. He had no knowledge of the silver they had received, nor did he know that Joseph's disappearance was an act of revenge. Unfortunately, the son who was suffering with him was the one he thought was dead. Revenge comforts the bystanders by pretending to be innocent. When others are silently suffering, revenge is silently rejoicing. Jacob was falling apart at the loss of his son.

"All his sons and daughters came to comfort him, but he refused to be comforted" (Genesis 37:35, NIV).

Whenever I teach on this story, I often joke that even the best among us has at one time or another thought about selling a younger sibling, but this was no joke. Slavery is a cruel and unusual form of punishment. Later, we are even told that the brothers had Joseph pleading for his life and that he was very distressed (Genesis 42:21).

Maybe you're reading this chapter and, like Joseph's brothers, you're staring down a hole that contains your enemies. Can you see their faces? Maybe a few of them have been in there for a while, while others are new arrivals. You didn't kill them, not yet anyway. Killing them was your first thought; now you just want them to suffer. You are punishing them with your words and actions until you can figure out how to get something out of it.

After all, they took so much. Did they think that you would just let it go? Are you Joseph's brothers? The plan, the hole you put them in, the counterfeit concern, all bring the corners of your mouth a little higher. They didn't see it coming, but you did. Have you forgotten the words of a man who truly knows what it is like to love and forgive his torturer?

"But I say to you who hear, love your enemies, do good to those who hate you" (Luke 6:27, ESV).

If revenge has built a house for you, consider making the next few pages your new address. This will be difficult, especially if the injury is fresh, but you can do it. Remember, your offender is an imperfect person just like you. Keep in mind that while you are staring down at them, it is very possible that if you look up, there is someone else staring down at you. It is sometimes difficult to see how our actions have hurt others, while it is easy to see how others have hurt us.

Revenge is blind.

Revenge needs a Seeing Eye dog.

It moves through life feeling its way. If you think about it, Joseph did not deserve the treatment that he received from his family. Sure, he did tell his father that his brothers weren't doing a good job with the flocks, but that did not warrant such extreme punishment. As far as we know, the robe that he received from his father was not something that he asked for. It was a gift. The anger it provoked should have been directed at Jacob, not Joseph.

When someone close to us enjoys an advantage that we secretly want, it can create a rift. The robe was the rift, but the dream was the icing on the cake. Telling the dream wasn't a good idea; it was, however, the truth. Joseph was only guilty of sharing it. The point is, revenge is blind to the facts. Revenge reminds us of how someone made us feel, and the result is it slowly eats away at our good judgment. The offense has a way of growing and becoming more ominous as time passes. I am not discounting the fact that occasionally someone will put you in a hole. I am only pointing out that some of your injuries aren't always a direct result of the person you have assigned blame. Like Joseph, they just happened to be the one wearing the robe.

Joseph, on the other hand, was intentionally and seriously injured. His life was completely turned upside down. In one day, he lost his home, family, and freedom, all as a result of what his brothers intentionally did to him. If anyone in this story deserved to get revenge, it was Joseph. His brothers deserved to be punished for what they had done. Just imagine going from being the favored son of a wealthy man to being sold into a foreign land as a slave. The robe of significance was replaced with chains of imprisonment. I am sure that Joseph was terrified and wondering what would become of him. He no doubt missed his family, even the ones who had put him in this position.

The time was coming when Joseph would have his opportunity to repay his brothers—to take his own revenge. When they saw him coming, they said, "Let's kill him." When he sees them coming, what would he do? Here is a clue.

"Do not repay evil for evil or reviling for reviling, but on the contrary, bless, for to this you were called, that you may obtain a blessing" (1 Peter 3:9, ESV).

Joseph was taken to Egypt and sold to a guy named Potiphar, who was the captain of Pharaoh's guard. The Lord was with Joseph and gave him great success. Everything that Joseph touched prospered. As a result, Potiphar put him in charge of his entire household. Potiphar concerned himself with nothing except for the food that he ate. Everything seemed to be working out until the day Potiphar's wife tried to entice Joseph into having sex with her. When he refused, she reversed the story and claimed that Joseph tried to rape her. Despite the good Joseph had shown all along, Potiphar was livid. He chose to believe his wife and had Joseph thrown into prison. Once again, Joseph was in chains for something that he had no control over.

There is no record of Joseph seeking or plotting revenge against Potiphar or his wife. He doesn't say, "After all I have done for you, why would you treat me this way?" He isn't silently churning out a plan to retaliate. It's becoming evident that Joseph is not like his brothers. While he is in prison, once again God is with him. And it wasn't long until the warden put him in charge of all the other prisoners. During his incarceration, Joseph gets a reputation for being able to interpret dreams, which will soon prove to be an advantage.

Revenge can be overturned.

Before long, Pharaoh begins having dreams that his magicians and wise men cannot interpret. The news of Joseph's ability to interpret dreams reaches the ruler. Pharaoh calls for Joseph to be brought from the prison. The dreams were explained; Joseph had the answer.

Joseph told Pharoah that seven years of great abundance was coming to the land of Egypt, followed by seven years of severe famine. He suggested Pharoah put a wise man in charge of all of Egypt. This man would collect a fifth of the harvest during the seven good years and hold it in reserve to feed the people during the seven bad years. Pharoah not only loved Joseph's idea, but he also put Joseph in charge of the grain collection. No one would be greater than Joseph in all the land other than Pharoah himself (Genesis 41:33-40).

Joseph did not waste his time at Potiphar's house stewing over what his brothers had done, nor did he waste his time in prison sulking over the false accusations of Potiphar's wife. He refused to so much as entertain the idea of revenge. His humility paid off. The one-time slave was now second in command of all of Egypt.

Revenge wants your future.

Revenge wants what's coming. It loves to take the position you could have had if you had not acted so hastily. More practically, life is full of people who walk around in chains that are connected to the past when they should be storing up grain for the future. Revenge takes your title. What you were created to be can get lost when you decide to get justice for yourself instead of letting God avenge you. Revenge is always testing us. Joseph's greatest test was still to come. His opportunity for vengeance was fast approaching.

At the request of their father, ten of Joseph's brothers left for Egypt to buy grain. The youngest, Benjamin, stayed home because Jacob was afraid that harm might come to him. The brothers were oblivious to the fact that Joseph was now governor of the land.

"So when Joseph's brothers arrived, they bowed down to him with their faces to the ground. As soon as Joseph saw his brothers, he recognized them, but he pretended to be a stranger and spoke harshly to them" (Genesis 42:6a-7b, NIV).

Just as predicted before they sold him into slavery, his brothers were now on their faces before him. The dream they had retaliated over had come full circle. Joseph was not yet ready to reveal himself, so he ordered that Simeon stay with him while the rest returned to the land of Canaan with the grain to feed their families.

If they were to return to get more grain in the future, they were to bring their youngest brother, Benjamin. This would be difficult, as Jacob was adamant about Benjamin staying home. Eventually the food ran out, and Jacob had no choice but to send his sons back to Egypt. This time, Benjamin went along. Upon their departure from Egypt, Joseph ordered his servants to place his silver cup in Benjamin's sack. As morning dawned and the men were on their way, Joseph sent a steward to go after them. He accused them of stealing the silver cup, an accusation they denied. "If it is found, the one who possesses it will be killed, and the others will become slaves," he told them. Each man quickly lowered his pack to the ground, and the cup was found in Benjamin's sack. The brothers were caught completely off guard by the turn of events and brought back to Joseph for judgment.

Every detail of this story indicates that Joseph is about to get his revenge. The silver cup was the last nail in the coffin. Now he can make slaves out of the very men who made a slave out of him. That is what revenge wants most—to be able to do unto others as they have done unto you.

"Chains for chains," revenge whispers. Joseph had a choice to make, and it's the same choice that you must make every time someone hurts you deeply. What will you do when your enemy is kneeling at your feet? Will you lift his head up or slice his head off? What did Joseph do?

> *Then Joseph said to his brothers, "Come close to me." When they had done so, he said, "I am your brother Joseph, the one you sold into Egypt! And now do not be distressed and do not be angry with yourselves for selling me here, because it was to save lives that God sent me ahead of you."* (Genesis 45:4-5, NIV)

Joseph told them to hurry back to their father, Jacob, and tell him that Joseph was still alive. He insisted that his entire family come to Egypt and live in the land of Goshen so that he could provide for them (Genesis 45:9-11).

Every time Joseph sent his brothers back home with grain, he returned to them the silver they used to pay for it. Now he is offering to allow them to live in the land of Goshen. Goshen is part of the Nile delta and was by far the most fertile piece of land in Egypt. Goshen is often referred to as the place called best. Instead of giving his brothers what they deserved, Joseph gave them his best.

Nothing ruins a good scandal like giving your best to those who treated you the worst.

All his life, Joseph made the choice to bless those who cursed him and treated him unfairly. As a result, Joseph's blessings in life far exceeded his tragedies. Instead of pouting and planning his retaliation, Joseph followed a different path.

Joseph's life teaches us that when we are treated unfairly, God can turn it around and use it for our good if we will resist the urge to get revenge. Joseph was looking at what happened differently than we typically do. The brothers sold him into slavery, but Joseph said, "God sent me." What the rest of us see as an injustice done to an innocent man, Joseph saw as a first-class plane ticket to his future.

Revenge doesn't trust God to use what you have been through for promotion.

Revenge cannot fathom that even when others put us on the bottom, God can shake things up until we come out on the top. God shook the prison until a dreamer became a powerful world leader. If God is allowing others to shake you up, it is not for the purpose of allowing you to make them pay up. God isn't looking to hire you to be His hit man. The purpose for the shaking is to keep you on track with your destiny. Even the things that aren't good are working for your good.

"And we know that in all things God works for the good of those who love him, who have been called according to his purpose" (Romans 8:28, NIV).

A few years ago, my life was shaken by Joseph's brothers. I wanted revenge so badly that I could taste it. Years of hard work and sacrifice were seemingly ripped from my hands, and there was nothing that I could do about it. I wanted retribution. I wanted to post it online and hang those who had wronged me from the clothesline.

As I wrote this chapter, I can now look back and see that what happened was working for my good. I could not see it at the time and would have argued with you until I was blue in the face that no good thing could ever come from the circumstance. However, the situation gave me the push I needed to move out of my comfort zone and begin my writing career. This book was brought to you in part by Joseph's brothers. They sold me to Egypt. I rose to the occasion! Will you?

"Dear God, I am sorry for the way that I have behaved. I am sorry for all of the nasty things that have been coming out of my mouth lately. I understand that hurting those who have hurt me will not make me hurt any less. I relinquish my rights to get even, settle the score, and make them pay. What they meant for evil, you can use for my good. Help me to leave the justice in my life to you. I want a heart like Joseph that says, 'What they meant to hurt me, God will use to send me.' Take my desire to retaliate and replace it with a heart that will bless those who have injured my spirit, in Jesus' name, amen."

REFLECTION QUESTIONS

1. Identify those situations where you're most likely to feel the need to retaliate. What different choice will you make next time you find yourself in a similar circumstance?

_____

_____

_____

_____

_____

_____

_____

_____

"Do not say, 'I will repay evil'; wait for the Lord, and he will deliver" (Proverbs 20:22, ESV).

2. Is it possible that what you feel has unfairly been done to you can be a door leading to a better place? Even if you can't see it right now, list some positive things that could happen as a result of what you've been through.

_____

_____

_____

_____

_____

_____

_____

_____

_____

"Jesus replied, 'You don't understand yet the meaning of what I'm doing, but soon it will be clear to you" (John 13:7, TPT)

3. Describe your place called best. What does life look like on the other side of the pit?

_____

_____

_____

_____

_____

_____

_____

_____

_____

"A thief only has one thing in mind—he wants to steal, slaughter, and destroy. But I have come to give you everything in abundance, more than you expect—life in its fullness until you overflow!" (John 10:10, TPT)

JEALOUSY

STICKS AND STONES AND ROTTEN BONES

"A calm and undisturbed mind and heart are the life and health of the body, but envy, jealousy, and wrath are like rottenness of the bones"

(Proverbs 14:30, AMPC).

"Resentment always hurts you more than it does the person you resent."

– Rick Warren, *The Purpose Driven Life*

Shakespeare was right. The green-eyed monster devours its prey without mercy. Jealousy locks in on what it perceives to be undeserved in others and feeds on what it cannot have. Like a raging bull, it gores the opposition. The horns come first. A gouge says, "I see what you are doing. Keep it up and I will trample you."

Jealousy sees the accomplishments of others as its own failure. Victimized by the prettier, smarter, and more successful, it simmers on low boil.

For you to get the most out of this chapter, you will be required to let down your guard and take an honest assessment of your heart. Unlike some of the other topics, jealousy wears a mask. It sits pew-side on Sunday morning, drives kids to baseball practice, and works in the most prestigious office buildings. It leads Boy Scouts, teaches community college, and works out at the gym. Jealousy is everywhere. It hides in plain sight. Like Solomon said, "You can't see rotten bones."

"A tranquil heart gives life to the flesh, but envy makes the bones rot" (Proverbs 14:30, ESV).

Jealousy doesn't care if you are family.

After Adam and Eve were banished from the Garden of Eden, they began raising the very first family. The king and queen of the earth birthed two princes, Cain and Abel. Both boys continued the family occupation.

"Now Abel kept flocks, and Cain worked the soil" (Genesis 4:2b, NIV).

Abel chose animals as a career path. Fittingly enough, Cain chose dirt as his profession. From the very beginning, the dirt wanted Cain. The mud under his fingernails held tight. He worked in the dirt, and the dirt worked in him. He was the first to be soiled by jealousy. King Solomon was very much aware of how powerful jealousy can be.

"Wrath is cruel and fury overwhelming, but who can stand before jealousy?" (Proverbs 27:4, NIV).

Jealousy doesn't care about credentials. It turns royalty into bowing servants. Even Cain, a son of Adam, was a candidate. For jealousy to work, it needs you to believe that when others are lifted, you are lowered.

Two brothers approached God. One brought something, the other brought everything. Cain brought some fruit, but Abel brought fat portions from the firstborn of his flock. The offerings could not have been farther apart. We can only imagine what Cain's offering looked like. Even the produce department at the local grocery store would have had a hard time picking through Cain's basket. Both offerings received a response from the Lord. The generous offering brought favor. The thoughtless offering was rejected. This made Cain very angry (Genesis 4:3-5).

The Lord questioned Cain's anger. He explained to Cain that it wasn't a mystery why his brother's offering was accepted while his was rejected. The Lord went one step further, telling Cain that sin was knocking at his door and that he needed to be the master of his own house (Genesis 4:6-7).

Jealousy plots before it attacks.

Just as the Lord warned, Cain opened the door to jealousy. As far as jealousy is concerned, the success of others is only a reminder of all the times it has been overlooked, shortchanged, and ignored. Instead of celebrating the fact that the Lord looked with favor upon his little brother, Cain resented Abel's success. Jealousy had all it needed. In Cain's mind, he was underappreciated, and Abel was overrated, proving that something doesn't have to be true for it to be true to you.

Maybe you can relate. The promotion you thought you had in the bag was given to the person three cubicles down. You lost twenty pounds and all anyone can talk about is the forty pounds your sister lost. Your pastor can't stop praising the new singer in the choir when you have been singing for ten years without any compliment. Jealousy will always be at the door knocking. No matter how much success you achieve in life, there will always be someone who you view as being more successful.

You can be the moon and still be jealous of the stars. Instead of admiring them, we can see them as an enemy. Cain was told to master his poor attitude before it became a sin. Jealousy unchecked quickly becomes a plan of attack.

"Now Cain said to his brother Abel, 'Let's go out to the field.' *While they were in the field, Cain attacked his brother Abel and killed him"* (Genesis 4:8, NIV).

The first murder in the Bible happened as a result of jealousy. Solomon was right when he said that jealousy is as cruel as the grave (Song of Solomon 8:6, KJV). The dirt wanted both brothers. Cain's actions were premeditated. Jealousy kills on purpose.

Jealousy attacks the innocent.

We are not told how Cain did the killing. Perhaps, as legend indicates, he used a rock. Since the name "Cain" is derived from a word meaning spear, it is my opinion he probably killed Abel with some kind of sharpened stick used as a gardening tool. Whatever he used was enough to wet the ground with blood, innocent blood. Jealousy loves to skewer the clean-handed. Consider this verse.

"By faith Abel brought God a better offering than Cain did. By *faith he was commended as righteous, when God spoke well of his* *offerings. And by faith Abel still speaks, even though he is dead"* (Hebrews 11:4, NIV).

Jealousy's victim is often innocent, guilty only of success. It is likely that Abel was killed in one of the fields where Cain grew his crops. Insulted, jealousy still kills in its own field. Whether at home, church, work, or the park, it doesn't really matter. Jealousy is territorial. Like a grizzly bear, we kill in our home range. Cain used a weapon. We use words. Those perceived as better than us become a shish kebab. The innocent—run though with forked tongues—never see the attack coming. Abel was only doing what God required when Cain took him down. Abel died once, but a jealous person dies every time someone else succeeds.

Jealousy will not allow you to rest.

Swift punishment came from the Lord. The ground would no longer yield its crops to Cain, and he would be a restless wanderer on the earth. Cain collapsed at the news, even telling God that the punishment was too much (Genesis 4:12-14, NIV).

The jealous never rest. They seldom feel at home or at ease. Something is always stirring them up. Cain said, "I can't stand this. The penalty is too high," but he never said, "I am sorry, help me change." Even when pleading his case to the Lord, his attention and focus were on himself. He does not mention his murdered brother; he only begs for a lighter punishment. When you are jealous and self-centered, you spend a lot of time thinking about yourself. The reason you can't rest is because you're always on your mind. James called this disorder.

"For where jealousy and selfish ambition exist, there will be disorder and every vile practice" (James 3:16, ESV).

The above verse says it all.

Disorder is exhausting. Chaos chases the jealous. Like a lion pursuing a wounded deer, it doesn't have to run very hard to catch those crippled with envy. Cain's life was about to change dramatically. Jealousy drove him over the edge. This time he had gone too far. There was no remorse for his unthinkable actions, only self-pity. The dried blood on his hands wasn't enough to jolt him to reality. Jealousy doesn't remember its victims. Cain was so fixated on how he had been wronged that he could not see what he had done wrong. That is precisely how jealousy works. We dismiss our ridiculous behavior; after all, in our minds, they deserved it. The result is a life of confusion and restless wandering.

"Then the Lord put a mark on Cain so that no one who found him would kill him" (Genesis 4:15b, NIV).

Jealousy leaves us marked.

Cain was a marked man. He was marked by God. Cain was forced to live in a land that no longer produced crops for him. For Cain, the only thing that came up from the dirt was the cry of his murdered brother.

"The Lord said, 'What have you done? Listen! Your brother's blood cries out to me from the ground'" (Genesis 4:10, NIV).

The jealous are still marked. Their actions have left them marked on the inside. Their dirt cries out as well, not for those they have treated poorly, unfairly judged, and been envious of, but also for themselves. A jealous person is deaf to the cries of Abel. Cain's voice cries out from their ground. The dirt screams, "What about me?"

Abel was guilty of nothing. He was a man giving his best, murdered by a man displaying his worst. His actions were righteous (1 John 3:12). The fat he gave wasn't meant to draw attention to him, nor was it a ploy to make his older brother seem lesser. Not everyone that you encounter in this life will be as righteous as Abel. Keep in mind that jealousy doesn't need perfection to be envious. It only needs you to get your eyes on the success of others. When the dirt starts to cry, pay attention to whose voice is coming up. Is it Cain or is it Abel?

Jude 1 talks about those who have gone the way of Cain.

"Woe to them! They have taken the way of Cain" (Jude 1:11a, NIV).

Have you taken the way of Cain? Are you dealing with a heart that is marked with jealousy? When others get the promotion, find a great spouse, drop the weight, or show up in a new car, do you smile to their face and glare behind their back? Jealousy is listed in the book of Galatians as one of the characteristics of our flesh.

Some of us struggle more with jealousy than others, just as some of us struggle more with sexual immorality than others. Jealousy can target you, as was the case with Cain. Remember, your flesh never gets saved. Even after your spirit gets born again and your mind gets renewed, you will still have to contend with your flesh daily.

Warfare is part of your walk. Jealousy may seem like one of the lesser works of our flesh but remember that it can and did lead to murder. According to Jesus, murder isn't always physical.

"You have heard that it was said to the people long ago, 'Do not murder, and anyone who murders will be subject to judgment.' But I tell you that anyone who is angry with a brother or sister will be subject to judgment" (Matthew 5:21-22a, NIV).

The way of Cain is the path of self-pity. When you walk in that direction, you will end up where Cain did. Your words become like spears and glances like gunshots. If looks could kill, you would give Billy the Kid a run for his money. You have taken the path many times, and it always ends the same. A friendship dead, a family member disowned, a coworker stripped to the bone with your jealous tongue. The ground is always bloody when you are a butcher.

Jealousy seldom gets better on its own.

Sometimes we think that our jealous tendencies are just a result of our immaturity and that when we get a little older, it will get better. Perhaps you feel that when you find a church that is a better match for your personality, you will spiritually move past your jealous nature. Both scenarios are unlikely. Unfortunately, there are even those who do not see their jealous personality as a problem. It's not their fault others are irritating. For you to get better, you need medicine for your rotten bones.

"Pleasant words are a honeycomb, sweet to the soul and healing to the bones" (Proverbs 16:24, NIV).

God has called in your prescription. Kind words heal rotten bones. If jealousy rots us, kindness cures us. A kind heart is warm, humane, and sympathetic. It invites peace rather than igniting trouble. It celebrates when others are celebrated. If jealousy is the disease, kindness is the cure. You may be thinking, "That sounds wonderful. Bring on the kind words, heaven knows I deserve them." I am not referring to how you have been treated in the past. I propose that this kindness is more in line with how you treat others.

Kind people do not have spiritual bone disease.

What a difference kindness would have made in this story. Cain could have kept his home and Abel his life. Jealousy cannot stand up to sincerity. If you struggle with the monster of jealousy, you will have to be intentional about ridding yourself of it.

"Whoever pursues righteousness and kindness will find life, righteousness, and honor" (Proverbs 21:21, ESV).

Kindness must become your pursuit for it to override jealousy. It will not be easy, as it is not your customary behavior. You may have been under its sway for as long as you can remember. That is why you will need help. Kindness is a fruit of the spirit. It is a natural byproduct of the fact that the Holy Spirit lives inside of you. However, it is still a behavior that you must choose daily. If the rottenness in your bones is to be cured, then you must take your medicine.

Jealousy must be nailed to the cross so that kindness can be resurrected. Even when your thoughts are clinging to jealousy, begin by using kind words. When you wake up in the morning, say, "I choose kindness today. I choose to rejoice with those who are rejoicing. I choose to see the accomplishments of others as a reason to celebrate. I choose to see the advantages enjoyed by my friends as their blessing instead of my curse. I choose kindness."

You no longer must go the way of Cain. You can go the way of kindness!

Jealousy is difficult to admit. After all, it seems so shallow. No one wants to own it. Jealousy is the ultimate form of selfishness because it puts so much focus on what we have decided we need in order to be happy. The acceptance of others only reminds us of our perceived rejection. This behavior has hijacked and sabotaged too many valuable relationships already. Stop feeding the monster. It's time to reject jealousy. Are you ready?

"Jealousy, I renounce you in the name of Jesus. I speak healing to my bones and peace to a mind that has been swayed by a spirit of rejection. I will no longer permit you to destroy my view of others and take my ability to enjoy their success. What others achieve is not my lack of achievement. I am beautifully and wonderfully made. Jesus created me to be enough! Jealousy, I replace you with kindness. Go now and do not come back. In Jesus' name, amen."

REFLECTION QUESTIONS

1. Resentment is often just jealousy in disguise. How does resentment most often try to creep into your heart? How will you change this?

_____

_____

_____

_____

_____

_____

_____

_____

"Celebrate with those who celebrate, and weep with those who grieve" (Romans 12:15, TPT).

2. Have you considered how much time you spend feeling overlooked and underrated? It is possible that the real problem is what you're telling yourself about those who sometimes enjoy what you believe to be an unfair advantage?

_____

_____

_____

_____

_____

_____

_____

_____

"Give thanks in all circumstances; for this is the will of God in Christ Jesus for you" (1 Thessalonians 5:18, NIV).

3. How can you practice kindness, especially to those you've been prone to be jealous of in the past?

_____

_____

_____

_____

_____

_____

_____

_____

"But love your enemies, and do good, and lend, expecting nothing in return, and your reward will be great, and you will be sons of the Most High, for he is kind to the ungrateful and the evil" (Luke 6:35, ESV).

UNGRATEFULNESS

PARADISE IS SELDOM ENOUGH

*"When the woman saw that the fruit of the tree was good for
food and pleasing to the eye, and also desirable for gaining wisdom,
she took some and ate it. She also gave some to her husband,
who was with her, and he ate it"*

(Genesis 3:6, NIV).

"There is so much good in the worst of us
and so much bad in the best of us, that it hardly behooves any of us
to talk about the rest of us."

– Anonymous

This chapter takes us to the earliest origins of humanity and, like the fruit involved, it is juicy and forbidden. A tidal wave of thanklessness washed over Adam and his wife that day. The original sin would drown us all. Usually, the snake gets the credit, but I propose more, much more. Ungratefulness leaves you standing in paradise, reaching for death.

I can't think of anything more confusing than what happened in Eden. It began with God's greatest and most excellent creation, mankind. Adam was the crown jewel of the earth. Even the sun in all its brilliance was denied the breath of life. God put his mouth in the dirt the day Adam was made. Lungs expanding and eyes flickering, the first earthling was waking up.

"The Lord God formed a man from the dust of the ground and breathed into his nostrils the breath of life, and the man became a living being" (Genesis 2:7, NIV).

Unlike a screaming, bloody infant being introduced to the world in the sterile environment of a hospital room, Adam woke up in paradise. The earth, as well as the garden, had already been formed. With his first breath, Adam could smell the salt in the ocean. His ears were filled with the crooning of songbirds. The colors of Eden's vegetation left him wide-eyed. Eden means "bliss" or "garden of delight." It looked like a page out of God's coloring book. The pristine paradise was perfect for Adam, but God was not finished.

God knew that Adam needed more than just beautiful landscaping. Adam needed a wife. So the Lord caused Adam to fall into a deep sleep. Once asleep, He took a rib from Adam's side and fashioned it into a woman (Genesis 2:21-22).

Eve wasn't just taken from Adam's side, she was also taken right out of his dreams! I'm sure that Adam and Eve began their lives together with the same enthusiasm as any newlywed couple. They had all the comforts of a nice home. They worked together. They oversaw the Garden of Eden and were to take care of it (Genesis 2:15). They didn't even have to do the laundry, for heaven's sake! What more could they possibly want?

Ungratefulness needs you to forget Eden.

The instructions were clear. If you want to continue living here, there is only one thing that is off limits to you.

"You are free to eat from any tree in the garden; but you must not eat from the tree of the knowledge of good and evil, for when you eat from it you will certainly die" (Genesis 2:16-17, NIV).

It is hard to imagine why anyone would even think about risking so much. The life that God had given Adam and Eve in Eden was exactly what we all claim to want. However, ungratefulness causes us to under appreciate what we already have and focus on what we don't have. Adam and Eve could eat from any other tree in the garden. You name it, any fruit, and it was there for the picking. I am sure that no matter which direction they looked, they could see branches heavy with choice fruits.

My favorite place in New York City is Chinatown. As a fruit lover, I am fascinated by the open-air markets filled with exotic and delicious fruits. My family and I like to walk past the overloaded carts and point out the vast variety of fruit that we have never heard of and cannot buy in Missouri where we live. Ripened to perfection, the foreign delicacies are very appealing. Before the snake could talk Eve into a bite of what she had never tasted, he would first have to take her focus off what she was already eating and make her curious about what the forbidden tree had to offer.

Imagine Eve, reclining on a canvas of lush green carpet. She has a fig in one hand and some almonds, still in their shells, are casually strewn about her side. A yellow rose tucked behind her ear keeps her ebony hair from hanging in her eyes. She can see Adam. He is naming the animals today (Genesis 2:19).

"What do you think about this one, Eve? I am going to call him a lion."

"I like that. It fits! He is so fierce looking, and that mane of his is magnificent."

"I know. I am glad he is so gentle."

"Adam, can we keep him for a pet? Please!"

"Eve, you know what Father said. We are only to name the animals. We must allow them to move freely about the garden."

For days they came, bird and beast. Adam named them all. Eden was a little slice of heaven.

Adam was not the only thing that Eve could see. She could also see a tree. It grew in the middle of the garden (Genesis 2:9). Its branches seemed particularly heavy today. Adam had spoken to her about the tree on more than one occasion. "We cannot eat this fruit, Eve. Father has prohibited it. If we do, we will surely die." Ungratefulness works its magic when we forget how richly God has blessed us. It causes us to look past all the fruit we are allowed to eat and fixate our attention on the one fruit that is forbidden.

Ungratefulness gets its power from the very things we feel our lives are lacking, especially when we blame God for keeping from us what we desire. Ungratefulness wants us to walk past orchards of abundance to hang out in a desert of death. To catch a glimpse of the forbidden tree, Eve had to look past the fruit she could eat. She began to get dissatisfied.

Ungratefulness offers you amnesia.

I know what you must be thinking. "My life isn't anything like the Garden of Eden and it is, for sure, not perfect." I concur. Life is seldom a naked picnic in paradise with your dream boat. It is, however, worth protecting. Becoming ungrateful for what you have is the first step to losing it. The Apostle Paul warned his young protégé, Timothy, of our ability to forget the blessings hanging like fruit all around us.

*"People will be lovers of themselves, lovers of money, boastful, proud, abusive, disobedient to their parents, **ungrateful**, unholy"* (2 Timothy 3:2, NIV, emphasis mine).

From the soccer mom who feels ignored by her hard-working husband and begins seeking attention elsewhere, to the average

American Christian living more lavishly than two-thirds of world's population, yet still complains about not having enough, ungratefulness is not hard to find. It shows us a forbidden fruit tree in the middle of our garden and says, "One bite. You deserve it."

As was the case with Adam and Eve, it is easy to become desensitized when living in the land of plenty. While it is not hard to see what we don't have, seeing what we do have is the real challenge. Ungratefulness requires intentional forgetting. Eve was ungrateful. Her short-term memory loss led to long-term ramifications.

I have thought about this story on many occasions. Formulating different hypotheses and trying to make sense out of what should have been a no-brainer only creates more confusion for me. What happened to Eve? Why did she make the choice to reach out and take the fruit?

As with most debacles, if we could see the end from the beginning we would run in the opposite direction. If we knew how it would turn out, we would not only avoid it, but we would also warn anyone within earshot of the dangers lying ahead. The serpentine path to the middle of the garden was deliberate. Ungratefulness can't walk a straight line.

A chill slithered down Eve's spine as she approached the middle of the garden. She had been here before, but it felt different this time. She was not alone.

"Now the serpent was more crafty than any of the wild animals the Lord God had made. He said to the woman, 'Did God really say you must not eat from any tree in the garden?'" (Genesis 3:1, NIV).

Ungratefulness diverts your attention.

An ungrateful person is always looking for loopholes. Their T-shirts read the same. How can I get more? The snake had Eve's attention. While God plants beautiful gardens filled with mouthwatering and savory fruits, Satan plants doubt and grows fear. Eve was not dealing with a first-time farmer. Satan's last seeds of doubt sprouted and grew until angels became demons. The stakes were higher now.

God was quick to point out to Adam and Eve all the trees in the garden they could eat from (Genesis 2:16). Ungratefulness was quick to point out the one tree they were to avoid. Eve usually gets the bulk of the blame, but the snake wasn't the only thing with her when she ate.

"When the woman saw that the fruit of the tree was good for food and pleasing to the eye, and also desirable for gaining wisdom, she took some and ate it. She also gave some to her husband, who was with her, and he ate it" (Genesis 3:6, NIV).

That's right. Adam was there the day the fruit peeled them both. Side by side the two ingrates wiped the forbidden off the corners of each other's mouths. It is unclear if Adam heard the conversation between Eve and the serpent. It is clear, however, that Adam was very much aware of what he was eating. He was no more tricked into eating the fruit than Eve was. It was not an accident. I am quite sure that the fruit on the tree of the knowledge of good and evil was very identifiable. Adam blamed Eve. Eve blamed the snake. I blame ungratefulness.

Eve saw the fruit and it was pleasing to her eyes. She may have been the apple of Adam's eye, but today she had an "apple" in her eye. The fruit that she didn't have had more of her attention than the fruit she had. That is the very definition of ungratefulness. It needs your full attention so that it can make you aware of all the things being withheld from you. Ungratefulness points out the curvy woman at the gym while forgetting about your marriage vow.

Ungratefulness drives up in a shiny new car that would put your family under a mountain of debt while forgetting about the great car in the driveway that you can afford. Forbidden fruit comes with both stems and strings.

Ungratefulness talks up the payoff and downplays the consequences.

Adam and Eve paid the ultimate price. Their eyes were opened, and they realized they were naked (Genesis 3:7). Paul described it best. Sin came into the world through one man, and death through sin, and so death spread to all men (Romans 5:12). The dirt kicked up would take us back to the dirt. Thankfully, Jesus came to undo what Adam and Eve's ungratefulness did to all of us.

"For as in Adam all die, so in Christ all will be made alive" (1 Corinthians 15:22, NIV).

Ungratefulness creates consequences. Eve's pain in childbirth was greatly increased. The ground that God commanded Adam and Eve to work became cursed with thorns and thistles. What previously grew without persuasion now required the sweat from Adam's brow. The original couple was evicted from the Garden of Eden. To top it off, Adam and Eve would be first to experience the sting of death with the murder of their second born son, Abel. What began as ungratefulness ended in a total loss.

The snake hasn't stopped slithering. He coils himself around the source of your blessing hoping that you, like Adam and Eve, will become ungrateful for all that the Heavenly Father has provided. "You will not surely die," he still hisses. Make no mistake about his motives. He is not interested in improving the quality of your life. Remember, the first snake didn't look like a snake. He is not an innocent grandmother offering you a piece of her finest peach cobbler. He is a dragon looking to reduce you to ash with false promises set ablaze by your own appetite for more. The Apostle Paul said it best.

"And no wonder, for Satan himself masquerades as an angel of light" (2 Corinthians 11:14, NIV).

I think one of the most valuable lessons we can learn from what happened in the Garden of Eden is that our blessings can become the source of our ungratefulness. Our fixation with what we can't touch becomes more dominant than the things we are allowed to snuggle with. Remember, snakes are not very cuddly!

We often pray for a new home that we can afford, and when we get it, it's never as big as the one down the block. Our blessing becomes the source of our ungratefulness. After all, we deserved the bigger house, right? It's not our fault that we couldn't afford a nicer one. Perhaps it's a car, job, or a spouse. Even though we are blessed with one, there is always something better out there—or so we think. What we do have only reminds us of what we don't have. All the fruit provided to us in the garden gets overlooked by the one variety that we can't get our hands on.

Ungratefulness has an appetite for destruction.

"All the toil of man is for his mouth, yet his appetite is not satisfied" (Ecclesiastes 6:7, ESV).

Solomon was right. We are never full. Like the Children of Israel standing in fields of manna, complaining because that's all there is to eat, ungratefulness is never satisfied. An insatiable appetite for more causes hunger pangs in stomachs already bloated from overeating. With ungratefulness, enough is never enough.

When I was a child, I was overweight and always on a diet. My mom lovingly said to me "Son, when you are full, stop eating." This is a lesson that desperately needs to be taught to those of us in the body of Christ. In many cases, we have forgotten how to be full.

Ungratefulness fears contentment.

What if Adam and Eve had been content with what God had given them, rather than obsessed with what the snake was offering? Would it have changed anything? The answer is yes. Paradise would have been saved and death would have lost. What if you could learn how to be content? Would that help? Of course it would. Like interest paid on an overdue credit card, our lack of contentment comes at a high price.

"Now there is great gain in godliness with contentment" (1 Timothy 6:8a, ESVUK).

When we are content with what God has entrusted to us, we gain. When we are ungrateful for what we don't have, we lose. There is a big difference between being content with what you have and being satisfied with what you don't have. Personally, I am never satisfied. I am always striving to be my best. Physically, emotionally, and spiritually, I want to climb higher every day. However, like the Apostle Paul, I am learning to be content in whatever situation I am in (Philippians 4:11). Satisfaction can breed stagnation. Contentment, however, moves us closer to godliness. You can reach for the stars without reaching for the forbidden fruit. A lack of satisfaction drives you to come up higher and be your best. A lack of contentment drives you insane and brings out your worst.

The lack of satisfaction wasn't the culprit in Eden.

Ungratefulness is what puts thorns on roses. I cannot buy roses for my wife without thinking about the first wife, Eve. The first bouquets were nonchalantly picked in the garden without regard for pokes and poisons. Eve didn't need gloves. Ungratefulness changed that. Thorns poked Eve's hands and wrist. Thorns poked Jesus' brow. Thorns poke our hearts every time we are ungrateful. Ungratefulness leaves us full of holes.

What is the snake talking to you about? You may not immediately know the answer to this question. Let me phrase it differently so that you can get the full impact. What is the snake trying to devalue? You know, what is he subtly suggesting is not enough? For Adam and Eve, it was a garden of delight. Perhaps it is your marriage, financial condition, job, church, or self-image. If the snake can get you to take your eyes off Eden even for a minute, great damage can result.

Maybe you are reading this chapter, and you can relate to Adam and Eve. You have walked past the fruit growing on the outskirts of the garden to the middle of the garden on many occasions. Good is never good enough for you. Great should have been greater. Even the best leaves you ungrateful and less than content. Your blessing has become the source of your ungratefulness. Restlessly you wander and constantly search for more. Problem is, more is never enough. You live in a state of irritation, and now you know why.

While being ungrateful is not a sin, it can lead you into sin. This character flaw should be treated like cancer. Remove it before it kills you. Jesus also offers you a tree. He was crucified on this one. The next tree you reach for should be cross-shaped.

"And those who belong to Christ Jesus have crucified the flesh with its passions and desires" (Galatians 5:24, ESV).

Ungratefulness has us reaching for the wrong tree.

Maybe you have heard of passion fruit. It is round, dark purple in color, and is often added to other fruit juices to enhance aroma. It looks and smells good but leaves a bitter aftertaste. The snake offered his own variety. Eve reached for the fruit. Jesus reached for the cross. Eve was ungrateful and wanted more. Jesus was content to do His Father's will and was willing to make Himself less. Ungratefulness never agrees to less.

Which tree will you reach for? Will it be the one with a snake hanging in it or the one with God hanging on it? Coils held the snake. Love held the Savior. Jesus is no longer hanging on the tree. Easter fixed that. The snake, however, still hangs out there.

While an ungrateful person can be a born-again Christian, it makes for a very disappointing life. Ungratefulness led to disobedience, which is sin.

"So whoever knows the right thing to do and fails to do it, for him it is sin" (James 4:17 ESV).

The second Eve bit into the fruit, she sinned. Ungratefulness was the path she took to the center of the garden. Ungratefulness has less to do with whether you will make it to heaven and more to do with the condition of your garden. Will your roses be with or without thorns?

Maybe you are reading this chapter and for the first time in a long time, you are realizing how ungrateful you have been. The Holy Spirit is stirring you and you know there is a snake in your garden. Like a spoiled child, you throw a fit every time something doesn't work out like you planned. Perhaps you have more than most, yet it is still not enough for you. Your spouse and your children have grown accustomed to your tantrums. No matter how good something is, you still find fault. Jobs, churches, family relationships, and even how you look only frustrate you. You are not high-strung, entitled, or different than the rest of us. You are ungrateful. Bring your ungrateful heart to the tree. The cross shaped one.

"Submit yourselves therefore to God. Resist the devil, and he will flee from you" (James 4:7, ESV).

Submitting to God means resisting the snake. Once ungratefulness is resisted, the snake will begin to lose his power. It will not be easy, and like any other character flaw it will require prayer, persistence, and accountability. I suggest you start with prayer. Whenever God finds a genuine heart that is serious about changing, He will partner with that heart. Once the Holy Spirit that lives inside of you is given permission to drive back the snake, change is the natural outcome.

Now that you realize your ungrateful heart is leading you down a path that ends in eventual sin and devastation, it is time to make the necessary adjustments. If you are serious about renouncing your ungrateful attitude and starting fresh, I invite you to confront your behavior and pray with me.

First, think about all the things in your life that are good. Make a list. Write out each one and add why they are good. Once you have your list in hand (see reflection questions) take a moment to be thankful.

"Always giving thanks to God the Father for everything, in the name of our Lord Jesus Christ" (Ephesians 5:20, NIV).

Second, consider the things on your list. Have you been ungrateful in the past for any of them? Which ones? What are you going to do differently now so that you don't allow the same behavior to reoccur? What will your guardrails be? The information contained in this chapter will be a great point of reference for you as you write out your battle plan.

Third, let's pray together.

"Heavenly Father, I have been so ungrateful for all blessings that you have given to me. Like Eve, I have paid more attention to what I don't have rather than being grateful for what I do have. I am sorry. Help me to see the good around me and to be content with all that I have been given. Remove the snake of ungratefulness from my garden. If I reach for a tree, let it be cross-shaped. In Jesus' name, amen."

REFLECTION QUESTIONS

1. Have you considered how you might be underappreciating what God has already blessed you with? Make a list of everything good in your life. Now, recount the reasons why those things are good.

_____

_____

_____

_____

_____

_____

_____

"Giv[e] thanks always and for everything to God the Father in the name of our Lord Jesus Christ" (Ephesians 5:20, ESV).

2. As was the case with Eve, has the serpent been whispering to you? Has he been portraying what God says is "off limits" as something that would enhance your life? How will you refuse his voice?

_____

_____

_____

_____

_____

"A thief only has one thing in mind – he wants to steal, slaughter, and destroy" (John 10:10, TPT).

3. How will you practice being content?

_____

_____

_____

_____

_____

_____

"So above all, constantly chase after the realm of God's kingdom and the righteousness that proceeds from him" (Matthew 6:33, TPT).

BETRAYAL

THE KISS OF DEATH

"Wounds of a friend can be trusted but an enemy multiplies kisses"
(Proverbs 27:6, NIV).

"The saddest thing about betrayal is that
it never comes from your enemies."

– author unknown

It looked like a scene from *The Godfather*. Overdressed thugs were looking to make an example out of a carpenter who claimed to be God. This outsider from Nazareth was bad for business. A kiss from a supposed friend, Judas, marked the target. The chief priests had to be sure, after all, there were eleven other men standing on the mountainside with Jesus (Luke 22:47-48).

We are not clear as to when Jesus first called Judas. His entry into the fellowship of Jesus' ministry team is shrouded in mystery. One thing, however, is clear. Jesus knew exactly what He was getting into when He added Judas to His staff.

The story of Judas has always intrigued me. Jesus wasn't nearly as stern with him as He was with some of the other disciples. When James and John wanted to call down fire from heaven to consume the Samaritans, Jesus gave them a stern talking to. When Peter tried to talk Him out of the cross, Jesus referred to Peter as Satan. As far as we know, Judas was never reprimanded in such an extreme manner. Why not? Perhaps Judas wasn't as terrible as he is usually depicted. Maybe he started out like the rest and just made some bad choices.

I truly believe that before Judas was a double-crosser, he was a disciple. Jesus would never have compromised the mission by adding a moron to the fledgling group. So what happened to this team player turned traitor? When did the banker of the group go backstabber?

A better question might be: have you gone backstabber? Have you broken trust, become disloyal and unfaithful to those who thought you had their back? Has Judas happened to you? This story is proof that even those close to Jesus can be swayed by the power of betrayal. For betrayal to work, two ingredients are required: offense and trust.

Betrayal knows what we want and creates an offense when we don't get it.

Betrayal has two triggers. Like a double-barreled shotgun, when both are pulled at the same time, there is quite a blast.

The first trigger has to do with what we want.

The second trigger is the offense that occurs when we don't get it. For Judas, it was money. He loved the feel of coins in his palm and the attention that came at the market when he pulled out much more than was needed. He loved money and the way wealth made him feel. Your trigger might be the affection that you are not getting from your spouse or the affirmation you feel you deserve from your boss. Perhaps it's respect you're after. Like Judas, it could even be something superficial like money. The temptation to betray those with whom we are in a trusting relationship is often rooted in offense.

When someone isn't giving us what we want, it becomes easier for us to turn our backs on them. We seldom betray anyone or anything that is building us up or meeting our perceived needs. Before Judas went to the chief priest seeking payment for the Messiah, he was offended. Before he betrayed, he balked. John tells the story.

The day Mary poured expensive perfume on the feet of Jesus; Judas objected. He made the argument that the perfume should have been sold and the money given to the poor. Judas, however, didn't care at all about the poor (John 12:4-6).

When Mary opened the perfume, Jesus smelled worship. Judas smelled cash—a year's worth, to be exact. The woman gave no thought to the cost as she perfumed the feet of Jesus. All Judas could think about was the money out of his pocket. Apparently, John had been keeping a sharp eye on Judas's spending habits. He makes a point to clarify what Judas really wanted. Judas wanted to sell fragrant oil and keep the money for himself. I believe this was the catalyst for his betrayal of Jesus. At the very least it gives us some insight into the thought pattern Judas used to justify his behavior. We find it easy to betray those who have offended us, from the husband who has an affair with a woman at his office because he feels offended by his wife's lack of interest to the employee stealing from her ungrateful boss. Offense makes us Judas. Mary was interested in anointing the Master's feet. Judas may have had his eye on the newest pair of sandals down at the local leather store.

An offense is all betrayal needs to move forward with its plan of vindication. An offended person feels like they have the go-ahead. Judas may or may not have started out like the other disciples, but he was losing ground fast.

"And Judas went to the chief priests and the officers of the temple guard and discussed with them how he might betray Jesus" (Luke 22:4, NIV).

Betrayal breaks trust and invites the enemy.

The temple may have been guarded, but Jesus wasn't. Not anymore. It only takes one soldier to break rank for the enemy to get through the line. Judas was the one. Betrayal happens when you are unfaithful in guarding your allegiance. Like Benedict Arnold, Judas changed sides. Betrayal sees those previously viewed as friends and teammates as enemies and offenders. It was a personal betrayal built around offense. Have you been there? Are you there now? You broke the deal to broker a better deal for yourself? You sat down with the opposition to discuss your options? Judas did it. We do it too when the offense cuts deep enough.

Judas went to the chief priest wanting to know how much he could get for handing over Jesus. He knew they were looking for an opportunity to take Jesus down. They counted out thirty pieces of silver (Matthew 26:14-16). The price was right for Judas. It wasn't a year's wage, but it was something. The silver reflected his face, but his actions reflected his heart. Once betrayal decides to break sacred bonds, it begins searching for just the right opportunity. Judas needed to get Jesus away from the crowds. The people loved Jesus and would never allow Him to be taken by force in the light of day. Jesus had a following and for good reason.

Betrayal does its best work when you forget who you are betraying. Judas was there the day the widow's son died. He watched as Jesus tapped the grave on the shoulder and said, "He is her only son. Let him go." Judas was there when the waters of Galilee became a carpet of blue, perfect for a God who takes long walks. Judas was there when a legion of demons said, "We know who you are. You are the Son of God."

Offense temporarily blocks our capacity to remember exactly who we are turning our backs on. While it may be difficult for you and me to understand how Judas could have betrayed the Lord, keep in mind, betrayal has selective memory. It allows you to remember the transgressions in the relationship without considering the positive benefits. You may see the person whom you are betraying in a completely different manner than everyone else. It can even become a source of irritation for you whenever you hear them being praised or bragged about. Judas was no longer a fan of Jesus. Betrayal happens when offense causes us to leave the fan club. Solomon knew and gave us this nugget of truth.

"A brother offended is harder to be won than a strong city: and their contentions are like the bars of a castle" (Proverbs 18:19, KJV).

Judas chose to betray Jesus. It was deliberate and planned. Betrayal is never accidental. Betrayal requires lots of forethought but not much afterthought. Judas wasn't thinking about the future. He was only thinking about himself. He never considered the brutality of the Romans, the cross, and the excruciating death Jesus would suffer. Betrayal doesn't think about how much pain it will inflict upon its victim. This concept might be easier to grasp if the victim were a stranger. But betrayal doesn't work on strangers; it needs a relationship to destroy.

"But the hand of him who is going to betray me is with mine on the table" (Luke 22:21, NIV).

Before Judas led the mob to Jesus, they had dinner together. Their hands may have bumped while reaching for the same piece of bread. The Last Supper is, without a doubt, one of the most famous and recognizable works of art. Leonardo da Vinci captures the moment perfectly. Thirteen close friends gathered for a meal. One of them was a devil. King David wrote about what would happen that night.

"Even my close friend in whom I trusted, who ate my bread, has lifted his heel against me" (Psalm 41:9, ESV).

Personally, I have never felt stabbed in the back by someone I didn't know. Backstabbers have to be close enough to reach you. Judas was close. Close enough to kiss. Betrayal isn't always aggressive. Soft kisses mark hard targets.

"But Jesus asked him, 'Judas, are you betraying the Son of Man with a kiss?'" (Luke 22:48, NIV).

Jesus knew the answer before He asked the question. Of course, Judas was betraying Him. There he stood, pockets lined with silver and supper stains still on his robe. All that was left to do was kiss the Master. A peck on the cheek led to thorns in Jesus' brow. Judas had approached Jesus many times in the past, but this time was different.

Betrayal has an agenda. Judas knew what the chief priest would do to Jesus once the Romans had their hands on Him. Betrayal isn't oblivious. The facts are in. Betrayal does its best work on those closest to us. The deeper the relationship, the deeper it cuts. Jesus was betrayed by one of His own.

I truly believe that when Judas began following Jesus, betrayal was the last thing on his mind. The relationship was what he wanted at first. His employer was both a carpenter and a God. He could create more than tables. He could create miracles! It was a dream job by anyone's standards. Betrayal doesn't happen overnight. Disciples do not become traitors in a day. Little by little, offense began chipping away at Judas. The incident at Mary's house put him over the top. He was the one who approached the chief priests and asked, "What's in it for me?"

Has there been an offense in one of your relationships? Have you been to Mary's house with Judas? Maybe you haven't led the chief priest to Jesus yet, but you have been thinking about it. You're upset. You want what you deserve. You have been telling yourself that others have been walking on you for too long and that it's time to finally do something for yourself. You can see the bag of silver, one coin for every day of the month that you get treated like a doormat. Your chance to get even is right there. You just haven't been brave enough to take it yet. You know where Jesus is. He is praying in the garden with the rest of his goody-two-shoes crew. You're just waiting for your opportunity.

Maybe I caught you just in time.

Betrayal offers a hefty payoff, but in the end, you pay an even greater price.

If given the chance, I would tell Judas not to do it. I would remind him that betrayal offers a bag of silver that soon loses its shine. I would grab his collar, look him straight in the eyes, and beg him to come to his senses. I would read him the end of his story and tell him it's not worth it.

Judas soon realized his mistake, but in his mind, it was too late. When he saw that Jesus was condemned, he returned the money to the chief priest. He told them he had sinned by turning over the Master, but they didn't care. Judas threw the money at their feet before leaving to hang himself (Matthew 27:3-5).

Judas had to have known the plan for execution all along. He was familiar with the Roman way of handling troublemakers like Jesus. Death by crucifixion was a common practice. Judas had seen more than one man take his last breath while hanging on a cross. He knew very well what fate waited for Jesus.

Betrayal doesn't think about the pain it inflicts. Betrayal has seen the devastating effects of what happens to the victim but conveniently dismisses them. It forgets the whip. The nails, what nails? The details get lost. When the ramifications of what he had done finally sank in, Judas was seized with regret. How could he have been so stupid? What made him think that the outcome could have possibly been any different? Betrayal painted an unrealistic picture for Judas. The canvas was convincing. "You will get what you want and somehow Jesus will come out unscathed." Betrayal still paints. It will show you the pastel colors of Easter while concealing red teardrops cried by old rugged crosses.

Once the fog lifted, Judas no longer wanted the very thing that he betrayed the Lord to obtain. The object of his attention was now the farthest thing from his mind. As a result, he returned the thirty pieces of silver to the temple. Betrayal loses its romance when Gods hang from trees. Betrayal offers a hefty payoff but, in the end, you pay an even greater price. What Judas had done was irreversible now. All he could do was repent and deal with the fallout.

Judas made a fatal mistake in his endeavor to reverse his bad choice. He went to the wrong source for forgiveness. Judas went the chief priest with his sin. He should have gone to Jesus instead. After all, Jesus was the one he betrayed.

The chief priest said it best, "What is that to us?" Judas felt the need to say that he was sorry, but his apology meant nothing to them. The chief priests were not the victims here; Jesus was. When a breakdown of trust occurs and a betrayal takes place, you have two stops to make.

First, unlike Judas, take your betrayal to Jesus. "I have sinned" is music to His ears. He will forgive you. Second, repent to the person you hurt, not to the person who helped you hurt them. Judas said the right words. He just said them to the wrong person.

When a betrayal takes place and the pain erupts, we are sometimes quick to tell everyone how sorry we are except for the person or persons who need to hear it most. The victim or the person we betrayed deserves an apology. It will not be easy to face them, nor will it be easy to own up to your embarrassing behavior. Do it anyway. Judas is proof that misdirected repentance is not true repentance.

When the circumstances around betrayal are mishandled, forgiving yourself will be difficult. After Judas left the temple, he did the unthinkable. Instead of forgiving himself, he hung himself. The potential world changer, miracle worker, and church planter came to the end of his rope. What he refused to make right ended in suicide. Suicidal people have lost all vision for the future. Judas betrayed before he believed life was no longer worth living. It is a heavy reminder to those considering betrayal. The story of Judas doesn't end there.

"The chief priest picked up the coins and said, 'It is against the law to put this into the treasury, since it is blood money.' So they decided to use the money to buy the potter's field as a burial place of foreigners" (Matthew 27:6-7, NIV).

Betrayal leaves us broken and scattered.

There is much debate as to exactly what this field was used for before they purchased it. Some believe the clay in the field was the perfect consistency for making fine crockery, while others are of the persuasion that it was a field used to dispose of broken pottery. I am inclined to believe the latter. All the busted pots in the world were not as broken as Judas. The fragmented pieces of what were once useful cluttered the ground like the shattered future of this traitor. The returned silver was used to purchase a plot of brokenness.

The potter's field was Judas. Fine pots that at one time served a purpose now lay in pieces in the dirt. What used to decorate someone's home now littered the ground. That was Judas. The ornate was obliterated. The once useful was all used up.

There is no mention of where Judas was buried. The graveyard of brokenness is my best guess. Betrayal finds us, offends us, and leaves us crumbled in the dirt. Betrayal loves the smell of mud and will use anything, including our own disloyalty, to drag us there. Judas found out the hard way that blood money doesn't spend very well.

"That is why it has been called the Field of Blood to this day" (Matthew 27:8, NIV).

I have a feeling that Judas, like the other eleven disciples, had walked past this very field on many occasions. No doubt it was nearby and obviously for sale. Perhaps there was even a sign. Reduced price! Make an offer today! The field wasn't the only thing for sale; so was Judas. Maybe as he was noticing the "For Sale" sign on this piece of ground, the ground also noticed the "For Sale" sign on him. Cheap prices! Silver accepted! Like the field, Judas could be bought for the right price. He settled for thirty pieces of silver when what he really wanted was Mary's perfume bottle. The dirt got him dirt cheap.

Betrayal causes you to accept less than you really want. The measly amount of money that Judas settled for failed in comparison to the King's ransom Jesus was actually worth. Betrayal gives discounts to the disgusting.

You, too, have kissed Jesus, haven't you? You led the chief priests right to where you knew he would be. You couldn't let it go. Could you? You didn't get what you wanted, and now they are paying for it. Not with money, but with the satisfaction you are getting by turning away from them. They didn't listen to you, treat you fairly, or meet your need. Now they are getting what they had coming all along.

"When they had crucified Him, they divided up His clothes by casting lots. And sitting down, they kept watch over him there. Above his head they placed the written charge against Him: This is Jesus, the King of the Jews" (Matthew 27:35-37, NIV).

Tragically, two men died, Jesus and Judas. Betrayal promises revenge but delivers regret, mountains of it. So much, in fact, that it has left you looking for a way out. Don't buy a rope unless you're planning on using it for climbing.

A resurrection was coming. Someone was coming up from the dirt. Someone was climbing his way past buried bones and Death's captain of the guard. The dirt would keep one man and lose the other. Jesus came back from the ground. Judas did not.

Who will you resurrect, Jesus or Judas? Who is making a comeback—the faithful or the fraud? Who will show up this week at your job? Who will cook dinner for your family? Who will be driving the car to church this Sunday? Will it be Jesus or Judas? Who is coming back? Will you allow betrayal to keep you buried in the Potter's Field or will you bring the silver back to the one you betrayed and come back from the dirt like Jesus? The choice is yours.

Judas was eventually seized with remorse, but not in the beginning. At first all he could think about was the payoff he had received for his betrayal. I bet you can relate. Initially it was easy. However, the collateral damage continued to build. It wasn't until the consequences began catching up to him that he realized how grave the situation actually was. It was no stranger whom he had knifed in the back; it was a friend. A friend closer than a brother, to be exact.

Betrayal destroys the unsuspecting. After all, you wouldn't do that to them, but you did. Judas needed remorse, not rope. By the time Judas realized he was engrossed in an avalanche of betrayal, he felt as if it were too late to make things right. It was not. It is also not too late for you.

"Let love and faithfulness never leave you; bind them around your neck, write them on the tablet of your heart" (Proverbs 3:3, NIV).

What if Judas had taken Solomon's advice and bound faithfulness around his neck instead of rope? It goes without saying that, like Peter after his denial, Jesus would have restored Judas' discipleship after his betrayal. Sadly, we will never know how the story would have ended if only Judas had come to his senses. The dirt took Judas, but the dirt isn't taking you. Not if I have anything to say about it! Restoration is closer than you think. Your story doesn't have to end in a field reserved for the shattered. The people you have hurt deserve the silver back. Take it to them personally with a sincere apology. No excuses, and no mention of Mary's perfume. Just an honest owning up to what you have done will suffice. People seldom refuse a genuine apology with an eye toward making it right. Tell them what Judas should have told Jesus, "I have sinned. I have betrayed innocent blood."

Now take the rope off your neck and pray with me.

"*I am sorry for the pain that I have inflicted upon those who weren't expecting it. Forgive me for accepting the silver. Offense, you must go, in Jesus' name. I will no longer justify my reckless behavior. I refuse to continue punishing the innocent. Others are not the problem; I am the problem. I am no longer Judas. I am forgiven. Take this sin and help me guard my heart in the event that it would try and return. In Jesus' name, amen.*"

REFLECTION QUESTIONS

1. Is there an area of your life where offense often tries to gain a foothold? How will you put a stop to any behavior that could potentially leave you offended?

_____

_____

_____

_____

_____

_____

"Don't give the slanderous accuser, the Devil, an opportunity to manipulate you!" (Ephesians 4:27, TPT).

2. Describe a time in your life when you felt betrayed. How have you dealt with the pain? Do you still harbor unforgiveness? If so, what will you do now?

_____

_____

_____

_____

_____

_____

"And don't sin by letting anger control you. Don't let the sun go down while you are still angry" (Ephesians 4:26, NLT).

3. Is there someone you have betrayed in the past? If so, are they still suffering from that betrayal? If you haven't, are you willing to go to them to make amends?

_____

_____

_____

_____

_____

_____

"Do your best to live as everybody's friend" (Romans 12:18, TPT).

LYING

GAME OVER

"Jacob said to his father, 'I am Esau your firstborn.
I have done as you told me. Please sit up and eat some of my game,
so that you may give me your blessing'"

(Genesis 27:19, NIV).

"The worst thing about being lied to is
knowing you weren't worth the truth."

– Jean-Paul Sartre

Why do we lie when the truth is easier? The story we spin eventually ends up spinning us out of control. The list of lies we tell is long. We lie to avoid negative consequences, boost our egos, avoid conflict, and get ahead of those we feel are less deserving. For some, lying is a profession. They have told so many lies they have forgotten where the truth begins and ends. Whatever the case, God hates lying (Proverbs 6:17) and we should too.

A few years ago, I watched the movie *Liar Liar*. It revolved around the life of a fast-talking attorney, Fletcher, who built his career on the lies he told. Fletcher was also constantly lying to his young son, Max, and even gave him a lame excuse for missing his birthday party. Max decides to make an honest man out of his dad, so while blowing out his birthday candles, he wishes that for one day his dad cannot tell a lie.

The wish comes true and in spite of numerous attempts to lie, all Fletcher can do is tell the truth.

Do the people in your life wish that you would stop lying? Have they come to expect less than the truth from you? Maybe you can relate to the kid in the movie and your greatest wish is for truth and honesty. You have been purposely misled and now you trust very few, if any.

When a story is woven together with lies, it comes apart very easily. The truth, however, is binding. Truth keeps the fabric of our lives tightly knit. It is no accident that truth is described as the belt in the armor of God. The belt holds everything together and in place.

"Stand firm then, with the belt of truth buckled around your waist" (Ephesians 6:14a, NIV).

A person who struggles with telling the truth moves from one chaotic situation to the next. Jacob was such a man. Before God made him into a great nation, he was a lying little brother. Before God can promote you, He must first be able to trust you. The level with which you can be trusted can be measured by how truthful you are with those in your world. God has no interest in reading your resumé, especially if you wrote it. God is reading your life and is paying close attention to your level of honesty.

Jacob and Esau were the twin sons of Isaac and Rebecca. Esau was born first, then Jacob. The birth was unusual in that Jacob was grasping the heel of Esau as the boys came forth. Even then, Jacob seemed to know the importance of the birthright.

As the boys grew, it was obvious that they were very different. Esau was a hairy man who loved to spend time in the open country hunting game. Jacob, on the other hand, was a smooth-skinned, quiet man who spent his days among the tents. Even their personalities were different. Esau was short-sighted and ended up selling his birthright to Jacob for a bowl of beans (Genesis 25:33-34), while Jacob had a close eye on the future. When their father Isaac was old and his eyes were so weak that he could no longer see, he called for Esau. Isaac had a request for his oldest son. "Take your bow and go hunting. Bring me the kind of food I like, so that I may eat it and give you my blessing before I die" (Genesis 27:3-4).

The blessing was very important. It was an oral contract between Isaac and the son who received it. It prophesied the father's intention in regard to future blessings and could not be reversed. It included abundance, power, prosperity, and victory over enemies. By rights it belonged to Esau, the firstborn son.

Liars need accomplices.

When the lie is far reaching and affects the future, an accomplice is sometimes necessary. Big plans of deception need more than one schemer. Jacob learned how to lie from his mother.

Rebekah overheard the conversation between Isaac and Esau. She quickly came up with a plan to ensure that Jacob would receive the blessing instead. She told Jacob to go out to the flock and get her two of the best young goats. She would prepare the goats the way Isaac liked and then Jacob could take it to his father pretending to be Esau (Genesis 26:6-10).

Jacob liked the idea but was nervous. His brother was hairy and Jacob's skin was smooth. What if Isaac became aware of the deception and pronounced a curse instead of a blessing? Good thing for Jacob, an accomplice always has a way around the truth. To calm Jacob's fears, Rebekah added to the lie. She took the best clothes of Esau and put them on Jacob. She also covered his hands and the smooth part of with neck with goatskins (Genesis 27:15-16).

If the lie were to be believable, Rebekah and Jacob would have to work together. Jacob lied but his mother "covered" him. She covered more than his hands and neck. She covered his story. She helped him deceive his father. Who helps you deceive? Who covers you with goat skin or, better yet, covers for you whenever you aren't being truthful? Do you have a Rebekah? Is there a goat skinner behind the scenes arranging the deception for you?

Lying is no game.

"Jacob said to his father, 'I am Esau your firstborn. I have done as you told me. Please sit up and eat some of **my game,** *so that you may give me your blessing'"* (Genesis 27:19, NIV, emphasis mine).

Jacob had "game" all right. So do liars. It is a game that they have played on more than one occasion. Rigged to deceive, the game board is designed to move them forward to the winner's circle while everyone else loses a turn. Jacob said it out of his own mouth. "It's my game. Now give me your blessing." Liars still play the game. They give no thought to those whom they are cheating and deceiving. Even those as close as brothers get played. Jacob's actions were intentional and designed to trick his father into giving him what rightfully belonged to Esau. The lying game had begun, and Jacob was making up the rules as he went. Just like in this story, when the questions start, a liar always has a ready answer.

"Isaac asked his son, 'How did you find it so quickly, my son?' 'The Lord your God gave me success,' he replied" (Genesis 27:20, NIV).

As is always the case, one lie requires a string of lies to keep the story straight. First Jacob lied about his identity. Then, when his father questioned the speed of the hunt, Jacob told another lie to keep the story credible. Isaac, like most of the men of his time, was no doubt a hunter himself. I have a feeling that Esau learned how to stalk and harvest game from his father. Isaac obviously knew that hunting takes time and patience.

I'm an avid hunter myself and have spent hours sitting in the timber waiting on a whitetail buck or wily old gobbler. I know from experience that immediate success rarely happens. The quick return of his son with the tasty dinner made Isaac suspicious.

The best liars know exactly what to say so that the story doesn't fall apart. As difficult as it is to believe, Jacob had the audacity to include God in his lie. He knew that his father trusted in God and he would believe that the Lord provided the easy dinner. Isaac wouldn't question the Lord's provision, and Jacob knew it. A good liar always adds familiar components to the lie that will make it easier to sell the story. Jacob didn't say, "I am just a great hunter" or "It was my lucky day." No, he inserted the familiar. Isaac was well acquainted with the Lord's faithfulness.

Can you relate? Are you close enough to your victim that you know exactly what to say in order to be believable? Do you spin the tale in such a way that it removes suspicion and doubt? When you play the lying game, it's a roll of the dice. Will they believe you or will they call your bluff? Those who play the game best, like Jacob, use preexisting facts to keep the deception going. The best liars avoid the hard truth and use the familiar to disguise what they are actually up to. After all, the familiar sounds right. Jacob is a perfect example of how to tell a believable lie. He didn't create anything new or introduce a foreign concept. His story revolved around his father's experience as a hunter.

A lie can sound wrong but feel right.

Isaac was not totally convinced by Jacob's story. He was blind, and even though all seemed to be in order, something didn't sound quite right to him. So he requested that Jacob come close enough for him to touch his hands. Isaac needed to be sure that it was really Esau he was blessing. In confusion he said, "I hear the voice of Jacob, but I feel the hands of Esau," so he blessed him (Genesis 27:21-23).

Covered in goat skins, Jacob's hands felt like Esau's. Even though it sounded funny, it felt right to Isaac. The story was as phony as the hair on Jacob's arms. It felt right, but it was anything but right. One of the surefire ways to recognize when someone is lying to you is to trust the voice, not the feel. You have probably heard the old expression, if it looks like a duck and sounds like a duck, it is probably a duck.

Jacob took every precaution to make sure that his story had the right feel, but the one thing that he could not change was the sound of his voice. If you suspect that someone is lying to you, listen to what they are saying rather than trust the environment they have created. Distracted by hairy arms, Isaac bought the story. The best liars always try to distract you with ambience. Later, we find out that Jacob even smelled like his brother (Genesis 27:27).

There is no limit to how far a professional liar will go to distract you from the real truth. Liars are all the same. The husband who tries to take the attention off that fact that he is two hours late by bringing a bouquet of flowers home to his wife and the boss who gives big bonuses to his employees when they know that something shady is going on are both examples of distraction.

The charade continued. Jacob finally secured what he was after all along—his father's blessing. The birthright paled in comparison to the blessing. If lying was the game, the blessing was the prize. Jacob had won, at least for now. Solomon knew that what you compromise to get, you will not keep.

"The getting of treasure by a lying tongue is a fleeting vapor and a snare of death" (Proverbs 21:6, ESV).

Jacob had barely left Isaac's presence when Esau came in with the food he had hunted and prepared for his father. Isaac explained what Jacob had done. Esau was devastated.

"When Esau heard his father's words, he burst out with a loud and bitter cry and said to his father, 'Bless me—me too, my father!'" (Genesis 27:34, NIV).

Liars are selfish. They leave before the crying starts. Jacob had no regard for what he had done to his brother. There was no apology or explanation. He acted as if nothing had happened. Liars are best at lying to themselves about the amount of pain they inflict upon others. Perhaps Jacob thought that Esau was stronger than he and that he needed the blessing more.

Maybe Jacob resented the fact that even though he stole the birthright, Esau was still the firstborn. Even with these clues it is impossible to know for sure. We do know, however, that Jacob was only interested in himself. Liars usually cannot see the truth in the wake of devastation. To them the truth is irrelevant. What matters most is what will benefit them most. The victims are expendable. Jacob's dishonesty completely changed the course of Esau's life. It should not have been taken so lightly.

Lying separates and invites retaliation.

"Esau held a grudge against Jacob because of the blessing his father had given him. He said to himself, 'The days of mourning for my father are near; then I will kill my brother Jacob'" (Genesis 27:41, NIV).

Esau was not about to let his little brother get away with what he had done. He knew that Isaac, their father, was old and that he did not have long to live. Esau's plan was to wait until after Isaac had passed, then he would take revenge upon Jacob. This move indicates to me that Esau loved his father. He did not want to inflict undue pain upon his family by killing Jacob while Isaac was still living. As usual, the one who gets lied to, like Esau, is the person trying to do the right thing.

When a lie occurs, it takes trust out of the relationship. Everything that has been said or will be said is now measured against the lie. While trust can be reestablished over time, Esau had no intention of rebuilding his relationship with his brother. Jacob thought that everything was all right, but retaliation was on Esau's mind. Once Rebekah received word of what Esau was planning, she sent Jacob to live with his uncle Laban. She told Jacob that once his brother's anger calmed down, she would send word for him to come back home (Genesis 27:44-45).

Rebekah was right. What Jacob had done, he had done to his brother. It was personal. Lying is a personal attack. Like a hungry lioness, it looks at the herd but picks only one. The target will feed her. She must isolate it and get it away from the rest. That's when the claws come out. Liars rip us to shreds. I think it's the lack of respect that cuts us so deep. The truth hurts but being disrespected hurts more. Lying sends a clear message without using words. It says, "You are not worth the truth."

Some of us lie occasionally, while others lie habitually. Whatever your level of lying, the Apostle Paul makes it abundantly clear that we have a choice to make when it comes to how we communicate with the people in our world.

"Do not lie to one another, seeing that you have put off the old self with its practices and have put on the new self, which is being renewed in knowledge after the image of its creator" (Colossians 3:9-10, ESV).

Like any other sinful behavior, lying is one of the things that you must deliberately avoid. When you choose to lie, it opens the door for the enemy. When you choose not to lie, it is evidence that the truth lives in you. If the truth sets us free (John 8:32), then lying incarcerates us. Lying is a self-imposed prison created by bars of misrepresentation. Jacob needed to get rid of Jacob. After years of running from his lying ways, Jacob finally has a faceoff with himself and a wrestling match with God.

Alone with what he had done, Jacob wrestled with a man until daybreak. The man asked Jacob his name. "Jacob," he answered. "Your name will no longer be Jacob. You are now Israel, because you have struggled with God," the man said (Genesis 32:24-28).

Jacob means deceiver, usurper, and liar. Israel means prince. Jacob lost his name and his old ways the night he wrestled with God on the banks of the Jabbok River. He went on to father twelve sons who would become twelve tribes. The tribes came together to form a nation. The nation of Israel started out as a lying little brother.

Lying may have given you a bad name. Allow God to give you a new one.

Once you are branded a liar, it can be difficult to escape the label. People are sometimes quick to forgive but slow to forget. If lying has become your identity, then you face an uphill battle. Thank goodness you can climb!

"A false witness will not go unpunished, and he who breathes out lies will perish" (Proverbs 19:9, ESV).

If words take breath, then a person who breathes out lies cannot tell the truth. Like a fire-breathing dragon, their words cook everybody. This warning is not to be ignored. A liar will be punished. Like Jacob, maybe you started lying when you were young. At first it was just a fib here and there, but eventually the little fibs became bold-faced lies. Lying was easier for you. This way you could manipulate the situation in your favor. No one would be the wiser. Now you have lied so much that you can't remember where the truth starts and ends. Mark Twain was right. When you tell the truth, you don't have to have a good memory. The truth is always the truth. A lie, however, is constantly morphing into something else. The details cannot be kept straight.

Some people have what I would call a lying spirit. They are the ones who wreak the most havoc. Our families, places of employment, churches, and mirrors are full of them. The Bible talks about this very thing.

"Then a spirit came forward and stood before the Lord, saying, 'I will entice him.' And the Lord said to him, 'By what means?' And he said, 'I will go out, and be a lying spirit in the mouths of all his prophets'" (2 Chronicles 18:20-21, ESV).

Do you have a lying spirit in your mouth? Do you use words not to communicate but to manipulate or, worse yet, disintegrate the people around you? Can you relate to Jacob the deceiver but wish you were Israel the prince? A new name requires a new spirit.

"But when he, the Spirit of truth, comes, he will guide you into all truth" (John 16:13, NIV).

The very same God who wrestled with Jacob is calling to you. He will be your guide as you learn to embrace the truth. Your name will not change, but your reputation can. When I think of Jacob, my mind does not go to the story of the stolen blessing. I think of who he became, not who he was. I remember him as the hard-working husband of Rachel and Leah and the father of an entire nation of people. Every time I see the country of Israel on the news or on a map, I rejoice in the legacy of this wonderful patriarch.

Jacob outlived the mistakes of his past and so can you. It would have made for a sad story if Jacob had stayed the same. Being branded a liar does not have to be your end. In fact, you can start right where you are even if you are caught in a web of lies. Isn't it time for you to start being completely truthful? Imagine who you could be if you could only stop being who you are? A prince would be nice, but being called believable would be better!

Close your eyes and see yourself as a different person. A trustworthy spouse, an honest sibling, a forthright salesperson, and a straight-shooting friend are all great images. Those pictures could be you, if only you would develop them. Jacob did not have to lie to Esau; it was his choice. Lying is always a choice. Confusion goes wherever lying goes. Tell them both to go away. Let's pray.

"*Dear Jesus, I am sorry for my reluctance to tell the truth. I no longer want to be known as the person that I am. I need a new name and new start. Help me. I want to make right all of the stories that I have spun for my own selfish benefit. Like Jacob, I choose this battle. Not because I am hurting, but because I have hurt others. Life no longer needs to be about me and what I can get by twisting the circumstances for my own desires. Forgive me for playing the lying game. I declare, game over! In Jesus' name, amen.*"

REFLECTION QUESTIONS

1. Describe a situation where you're sometimes tempted to be less than honest. Ask yourself: Where am I located? Who am I with? What am I doing?

_____

_____

_____

_____

_____

_____

_____

"Don't lie to each other, for you have stripped off your old sinful nature and all its wicked deeds" (Colossians 3:9, NLT).

2. If you believe someone is lying to you, how will you listen to what is actually being said rather than trusting the environment of falsehood that is being created?

_____

_____

_____

_____

_____

_____

_____

_____

_____

"Know this, my beloved brothers; let every person be quick to hear, slow to speak, slow to anger" (James 1:19, ESV).

3. Is it possible that you are currently lying to yourself about a situation that others have been clearly warning you about? Is there an area where you refuse to see the truth?

_____

_____

_____

_____

_____

_____

_____

_____

"For all that is secret will eventually be brought into the open, and everything that is concealed will be brought to light and made known to all" (Luke 8:17, NLT).

GREED

JUST A LITTLE MORE

"Over Achan they heaped up a large pile of rocks which remains to this day. Then the Lord turned from his fierce anger"

(Joshua 7:26a, NIV).

"Greed scandalizes the soul. It takes what it doesn't need and needs what it doesn't take."

– Larry Dugger

In 1960, Bernie Madoff was a rookie penny stock trader. He started his fledgling investment firm with the five thousand dollars he earned working as a lifeguard and sprinkler installer. When it came to investing, Bernie seemed to be a natural, and as a result, he added several family members to his staff. His younger brother, Peter, was senior marketing director. Peter's daughter, Shana, was compliance attorney. Bernie's two sons, Mark and Andrew, worked in the trading section along with one of their cousins, Charles. Everything was champagne wishes and caviar dreams, until the truth came out.

On December 11, 2008, Bernie's sons first broke the story when they alerted law enforcement. Their father was operating the largest accounting scheme in American history. Prosecutors later estimated the value of the fraud to be in excess of 64 billion dollars, based on the accounts of Madoff's 4,800 clients. On June 29, 2009, Madoff was sentenced to 150 years in prison and ordered to pay back 17 billion in restitution. Exactly two years after the arrest of his father, Mark, Bernie's youngest son, committed suicide.

Thousands of investors lost everything, including retirement funds. Madoff made off with more than money. He took the future to prison with him. The once-lifeguard took everyone under, including his family. Greed looks out for itself. On Valentine's Day the card reads, "To me, my greatest love."

Greed can be a result of success.

Once the Children of Israel finally crossed the Jordan River and entered into the Promised Land, the first item of business was to take the city of Jericho. Jericho means moon-cry. It is very probable that this city was the epicenter of worship for the moon god. If they could defeat Jericho, it would send a strong message to the rest of pagan people living in Canaan. The Children of Israel were no joke, and their God was not to be taken lightly. Taking Jericho, however, would not be an easy task. Famous for its thick walls and formidable army of fighting men, it was nothing to sneeze at. If they were to succeed, they needed the Lord's help.

"Now the gates of Jericho were securely barred because of the Israelites. No one went out and no one came in. Then the Lord said to Joshua, 'See, I have delivered Jericho into your hands, along with its king and its fighting men" (Joshua 6:1-2, NIV).

The Lord was ready to come to the aid of His people, but there were conditions. Most if not all of God's promises come with conditions. The things God requires from His people are very purposeful and designed to keep us on course as we move through life. Without conditions, our decisions and behavior can get out of control. God does this for our benefit, not His. The conditions here were very straightforward.

First, they were to march around the city for seven days and on the seventh day, shout. This would bring the walls down (Joshua 6:3-5). Second, all the treasure of the city was not to be kept by individuals but put in the Lord's treasury. The Lord was clear.

"All the silver and gold and the articles of bronze and iron are sacred to the Lord and must go into his treasury" (Joshua 6:19, NIV).

Portions of this story remind me of the little country church I attended as a child. Marching grandmas shouted and sang while the praise band blew the trumpets. "Some glad morning when this life is o'er, I will fly away." I expected them to take flight at any moment! It's a wonderful memory. We need more marching grandmas.

Joshua and the people marched, and on the seventh day, the walls of the city fell. Only Rahab, the prostitute, and those in her house were spared. Everyone else was killed and all the spoil was put in the Lord's treasury. Or was it?

The next city on the list to be conquered was very small compared to Jericho. Ai should have been an easy target. Its walls were far less fortified than Jericho and there weren't nearly as many fighting men. Joshua only sent a fraction of his army to deal with the conquest, but it did not go as planned.

Something went terribly wrong. Even though 3,000 Israelite warriors went up, they were overtaken by a handful of men from

Ai, who killed 36 of them. The Israelites were chased from the city gate and struck down, causing the people's hearts to melt like water (Joshua 7:4-5). The Lord was not with Israel in this fight. Joshua was distraught concerning the Lord's absence. He fell before the Ark of the Covenant and asked the Lord why. The Lord quickly responded. He told Joshua that Israel had sinned and violated the covenant. The Lord explained how some of the things devoted to Him had been stolen and placed within the Israelite camp. *"This is why the Israelites cannot stand against their enemies ... I will not be with you anymore until you destroy whatever among you is devoted to destruction"* (Joshua 7:10-12).

The verdict was in. Greed was in the camp. Greed stole, lied, and coveted what it had no right to. One of the Jericho marchers turned moocher. Greed found a participant. Someone with an extreme desire to acquire took what did not belong to them. Who would do such a thing? Who would put an entire nation at risk in the pursuit of possessions? Bernie Madoff was not the first to be influenced by greed.

Tribe by tribe, clan by clan, and family by family, Israel came forward. Joshua with the help of the Lord was able to identify the perpetrator.

His name was Achan. Like Joshua and Jesus, Achan was from the tribe of Judah. Greed isn't interested in your ancestry. Achan's ancestral line was full of purebred champions. New Testament saviors and Old Testament sword swingers embodied his lineage. What began as the successful conquest of Jericho ended up in complete disaster. As is often the case with greedy people, Achan did not own up to what he had done until there were consequences. He was not sorry for his actions. He was sorry that God noticed them. He was caught, and there was no denying what he had done.

I can see Achan standing in front of Joshua. His hands were in his pockets, his eyes fixed on the ground. A bead of sweat ran down the side of his face. He knew what was coming but waited to be asked the question before he spoke. Joshua demanded an answer.

He wanted to know exactly what Achan had done (Joshua 7:19).

> *Achan replied, "It is true! I have sinned against the Lord,*
> *the God Israel. This is what I have done. When I saw*
> *in the plunder a beautiful robe from Babylonia, two*
> *hundred shekels of silver and a bar of gold weighing fifty*
> *shekels, I coveted them and took them. They are hidden*
> *in the ground inside my tent, with the silver underneath."*
> (Joshua 7:20-21, NIV)

When the nation of Israel left the bondage of Egypt in pursuit of Canaan, they departed with plunder in hand. The Egyptians didn't just allow them to leave, they gave them their wealth as they went. That should have been enough for Achan, but greed never has enough. Achan said it best, "I coveted them." Even though the Lord had forbidden it, the voracity to take overwhelmed him. Greed forgets what it already possesses and diverts your attention to the excessive. It doesn't know the definition of enough. Achan had no need for the things that he took. He simply wanted them for himself. The robe, silver, and gold were too wonderful to resist, and no one would ever have to know.

What could possibly go wrong?

Greed doesn't realize the devastating consequences of never having enough.

After he was cornered and could no longer lie about what he had done, Achan finally confessed. "It's true, I did it," he said. His confession was as little as it was late.

If he had actually felt remorse, he would have come forward when thirty-six soldiers from Israel were killed at Ai and his leader, Joshua, was lying on his face before the Ark trying to figure out what went wrong. Men died because of Achan's actions, and who knows how many more innocent lives would have been lost if Joshua had not recognized the bigger problem.

Joshua was face down on the ground before the Ark of the Lord. He knew something was wrong. Achan also had his face to the ground as he buried what he took, only there was no Ark and no thought of the Lord. There was only a hole full of treasure underneath his tent that he hoped no one would find out about. Greed digs a hole that eventually becomes a grave. Once again, buried in the dirt is where we find the dirt.

The dirt held his secrets.

The Lord was very specific about what had to happen next. There were no plea bargains or deals cut and no lawyers to lighten the sentence. What greed had taken had to be removed. He said to Joshua, "I will not be with you anymore until you remove the items devoted to destruction."

Greed is still devoted to destruction. Your destruction, that is. Greed is an endless effort to satisfy a desire without ever reaching satisfaction. It slowly consumes you until there is nothing left except for two reaching hands. It says, "Just a little more, and I will be content." The contentment it gains by gaining more never lasts. Like a hungry baby, greed cries, "Feed me."

"So Joshua sent messengers, and they ran to the tent, and there it was, hidden in his tent, with the silver underneath. They took the things from the tent, brought them to Joshua and all the Israelites and spread them out before the Lord" (Joshua 7:22-23, NIV).

There it was, spilled out on the ground before an entire nation. The scandal was full blown. Achan was at fault. Thirty-six grieving widows stared at the man who robbed them of the future. Their husbands died, not because Ai was strong, but because Achan was weak. Then, like now, those who lack self-control usually put others in the crosshairs. For greed to rise, the innocent often fall.

I think it is worth noting that Achan felt the need to hide the treasure he had coveted from his family. No one was allowed to know what he was doing. Greed is a secret hoarder. It stores its stash in dark corners and offshore bank accounts. It collects its treasure undetected and below the radar. What Achan worked so hard to bury soon buried him. Joshua took Achan, the silver, the robe, and the gold bar, his sons, his daughters, and all that he owned to the Valley of Achor. There they stoned him and his entire family. Afterward, they burnt everything (Joshua 7:24-25).

Achan was far from in need. In fact, everything indicates that he was very successful. Not only did he have a home, he had a great number of herds and flocks. He was obviously a married man with many children. It would have been easier to understand why he took the treasure out of Jericho if he were poor and trying to feed his family. The above verses are proof that his robbery of the Lord's treasury was not about need.

Greed is the inordinate desire to possess something with the intention of keeping it all for yourself. The robe was not a birthday present for his brother-in-law. The silver and gold were not meant for his children's college fund. Achan saw them, wanted them, and took them for himself. It was that simple.

"Whoever is greedy for unjust gain troubles his own household" (Proverbs 15:27, ESV).

Everything in Achan's world, right down to the smallest lamb, was rocked by greed. When greed is finished there is only a pile of rocks where once lived a thriving family. This story is a harsh reminder of what can happen when greed is not properly dealt with. If you are going to hide a treasure, make sure it's the right one. Jesus explains.

"The kingdom of heaven is like a treasure hidden in the field, which a man found and covered up. Then in his joy he goes and sells all that he has and buys that field" (Matthew 13:44, ESV).

True treasure hunters recognize something valuable when they see it. Once real treasure is identified, there are no lengths that they will not go to in order to secure it. Tens of thousands of dollars are spent in the recovery effort. The rarer and more unique the treasure, the more money invested. The kingdom of God is such a treasure. It cannot be imitated or duplicated. It is authentically priceless. Real treasure hunters are looking for Jesus. His kingdom is what they desire most. They would gladly give up all earthly possessions if the King requested it.

Greed hunts treasure for all the wrong reasons. Its objective is to show up in a new robe, wearing a gold chain. It never shares what it has. Greed parts with nothing. Greed gets what it can, cans what it can get, and sits on that can! Achan was a treasure hunter; too bad he wasn't looking for the right kind of treasure. His kingdom was more important to him than the kingdom of God. He was more interested in protecting what he had taken than he was in protecting his own family.

Greed was his god.

Greed is not always easy to identify.

What kind of treasure are you after? Is it Kingdom treasure or earthly treasure? Do you have anything buried beneath your tent? Something that you didn't need but you just had to have, and you didn't care who you hurt to get it. Perhaps you can relate to Achan. Maybe you have never thought of yourself as a greedy person, yet you have more than one Babylonian robe hanging in your closet. Greed isn't always easy to spot. It's not always dressed in an Armani suit. Sometimes it's dressed like a farmer from the tribe of Judah, a school bus driver from Texas, or a janitor from Cleveland. Greed looks like the rest of us.

While money and wealth are usually the elephants in the room when it comes to greed, you can be greedy for many things. Time, attention, praise, and the approval of others definitely make the list. Achan couldn't keep his behavior buried for long and you won't be able to either. Joshua dug it up. Someone always digs it up. It is only a matter of time.

"Over Achan they heaped up a large pile of rocks, which remains to this day" Joshua (7:26a, NIV).

A monument of greed still stands. Achan rocked the Israelites before they rocked him.

Achan might as well have been digging his own grave when he put the stolen treasure in the ground. If you are digging your own grave, you can stop at any time. It doesn't have to end in a pile of rocks. You can stop the runaway train before it crashes through the guardrails. It's never too late.

Greed scans the crowd, looking for a lack of contentment.

"Be content with what you have, for he said, "I will never leave you or forsake you"" (Hebrews 13:5b, ESV).

Success is not greed. Having a nice robe, a gold chain, or some new silver earrings is nothing to be ashamed of. In fact, success can be a sign that we are honoring God with our possessions. After all, when you steward your finances well, God says, *"I will … throw open the floodgates of heaven and pour out so much blessing that there will not be room enough to store it"* (Malachi 3:10, NIV).

I want my life to be filled with whatever God is throwing out of His windows! As the father of two teenage sons, nothing gives me more pleasure than to bless them when they honor my house with good character and behavior. God also gets pleasure from blessing his children. A successful Christian is not the same as a greedy Christian.

The problem wasn't the robe, gold, or silver. The problem was Achan's lack of contentment. As we've already discussed in a previous chapter, Adam and Eve also struggled in this area. While they wanted the forbidden fruit, Achan wanted personal treasure that no one would ever know about. Later, when the Children of Israel finally defeated Ai, God told them this time you can have the plunder (Joshua 8:2). If Achan had been content and only waited, he could have had much more than he took. If greed is the poison then contentment is the antidote. Greed is never feeling content with the nice things that you have.

Contentment is enjoying what God has given you to be steward over while you are on the earth. When you are happy and found faithful with what you have been given, God will give you more to enjoy. Greed, on the other hand, can't enjoy anything because it always has its eye on something else. Greed cannot be trusted with more because more never satisfies it. Achan may or may not have been godly, but one thing is for sure, he was not content.

What about you? Do you constantly "Ache" for more? Is enough never enough for you? In life it is usually not a good idea to play "What If," but in this case it might prove to be of value. What if Achan had thought it through and realized that he didn't need the stolen treasure to be happy? What if he took his greed to the Lord instead of taking it to the bank?

Greed cannot compete with contentment.

Greed loses its power when contentment shows up. If greed is superman, contentment is kryptonite. Contentment renders greed helpless. Perhaps the problem is you just haven't learned how to be content. Maybe you were raised in a home where excessive hoarding was considered normal. Perhaps you had very little as a child and now you are driven to get as much as you can get your hands on. It could be that greed is just the weak link in your spiritual armor. When tempted by greed, you will do well to have some ammunition in your arsenal. I can think of two valuable bullet points.

First, remember the words of Jesus. *"For one's life does not consist in the abundance of his possessions"* (Luke 12:15b, ESV).

Life is not about what you have. The real issue is, who has you? Do you belong to the treasure or the treasurer?

Second, keep in mind why you already have enough.

"A Psalm of David. The Lord is my shepherd; I shall not want" (Psalm 23:1, ESV).

When you realize that you have the God of everything, you need nothing. The Shepherd was David's source for not wanting. God provided all that David needed. Achan thought he needed the treasure. David knew that God was the treasure. If you are not content and you struggle with always wanting more, why not ask God to help?

Treat your lack of contentment just like you would anything else you struggle with. Approach Jesus and tell him how you feel and what you need. Ask in His name, for there is no greater power. He will do the internal work, and all you have to do is just show up with a sincere heart. You don't have to lose everything that you have in a quest to get more than you need. Life doesn't have to end in a pile of rocks. When rocked by greed, pick up the stone and throw it back. You don't need it! If you truly want to rid yourself of Achan's ache for more, pray with me.

"Dear Jesus, I am sorry for allowing greed to capture my heart. I ask you to forgive me my covetousness. Help me to be content with what I have been given. I refuse to allow what I do not have to become more important to me than what I do have. You are my shepherd and from this day forward, I shall not want. Greed, go, and contentment, come, in Jesus' name, amen."

REFLECTION QUESTIONS

1. Can you identify any situation in life where you tend to push for more than you need? A place where you "ache" to constantly have more?

_____

_____

_____

_____

_____

_____

_____

"And my God will supply every need of yours according to his riches in glory in Christ Jesus" (Philippians 4:19, ESV).

"I am convinced that my God will fully satisfy every need you have, for I have seen the abundant riches of glory revealed to me through Jesus Christ!" (Philippians 4:13, TPT)

2. In your opinion, what is the difference between earthly treasure and kingdom of God treasure?

_____

_____

_____

_____

_____

_____

_____

_____

"Blessed be the God and Father of our Lord Jesus Christ, who has blessed us in Christ with every spiritual blessing in the heavenly places" (Ephesians 1:3, ESV).

3. Success is not greed. Write out some of the way that God has blessed you. Now pause and take a minute to thank Him for those blessings.

_____

_____

_____

_____

_____

_____

_____

"Delight yourself in the Lord, and he will give you the desires of your heart" (Psalm 37:4, ESV).

"Make God the utmost delight and pleasure of your life, and he will provide for you what you desire the most" (Psalm 37:4, TPT).

CONCLUSION

As I sit and reflect on the content of this book, I'm reminded of all the times in my fifty years of life when I've made a bad choice. Most of my poor decisions were accidental, but if I'm being completely honest, some of my less-than-stellar behavior was done on purpose. I knew that what I was doing would end messily, and despite the gentle nudging of the Holy Spirit, I pressed ahead anyway. The truth is, each chapter of this book could easily reflect a chapter of my life. That's hard to admit, especially since God has entrusted me to speak into the hearts of thousands of people through teaching and writing each week. My hope is that by being honest, you can learn from my mistakes and avoid some of the fallout that I've had to endure.

No matter where you find yourself in life, I want you to know God truly has helped me overcome my worst decisions. And He will help you as well. As I closed each chapter, I prayed for you, and now that you've read though the material, my hope is that you are well equipped to recognize when a bad choice taps your shoulder. If you're still dealing with the fallout of a poor decision, remember, your identity is not in the worst thing you have ever done (nor is it in the best thing you have ever done). Your identity is found in Christ. The Apostle Paul was right. "It is no longer I who live, but

Christ who lives in me." Allow the Christ who lives in you to rise to the top!

Sometimes really good people (like you and me) make bad choices. Thankfully, we have a perfect God who never turns His back and is willing to walk hand in hand with us through the messiness of life—even when we invited the chaos. Keep going, my friend. You'll be glad you did.

ENDNOTES

Chapter One
"Like Water for Chocolate Quotes by Laura Esquivel." Goodreads. Accessed June 14, 2023. https://www.goodreads.com/work/quotes/1172473-como-agua-para-chocolate.

Chapter Two
"40 Quotes About Worldliness." ChristianQuotes. Last modified December 29, 2015. https://www.christianquotes.info/quotes-by-topic/quotes-about-worldliness/.

Chapter Three
"A Quote by George Harrison." Goodreads. Accessed June 14, 2023. https://www.goodreads.com/quotes/7450671-gossip-is-the-devil-s-radio-don-t-be-a-broadcaster.

Chapter Four
"Top 30 COVER UPS Quotes and Sayings." Inspiring Quotes. Last modified June 10, 2023. https://www.inspiringquotes.us/topic/7409-cover-ups.

Chapter Six
"27 Quotes About Self-love." ChristianQuotes. Last modified December 29, 2015. https://www.christianquotes.info/quotes-by-topic/quotes-about-self-love/.

Anderson, Hans Christian. "The Emperor's New Clothes." Fairy Tales and Other Traditional Stories. Lit2Go: Florida Center for Instructional Technology. Accessed August 22, 2023. https://etc.usf.edu/lit2go/68/fairy-tales-and-other-traditional-stories/5637/the-emperors-new-clothes/.

Chapter Seven
"Joel Osteen Quotes." BrainyQuote. Accessed June 14, 2023. https://www.brainyquote.com/quotes/joel_osteen_5790.

Chapter Eight
"The Purpose Driven Life Quotes by Rick Warren." Goodreads. Accessed June 14, 2023. https://www.goodreads.com/work/quotes/2265235-the-purpose-driven-life-what-on-earth-am-i-here-for.
"The Green-eyed Monster." ENotes. Accessed June 14, 2023. https://www.enotes.com/shakespeare-quotes/o-beware-my-lord-jealousy.

Chapter Nine
"A Quote by Edgar Evans Cayce." Goodreads. Accessed June 14, 2023. https://www.goodreads.com/quotes/51185.

Chapter Ten
" Bible Verses About Betrayal." Bible Reasons. Last modified May 22, 2023. https://biblereasons.com/betrayal/.

Chapter Eleven
"A Quote by Jean-Paul Sartre." Goodreads. Accessed June 14, 2023. https://www.goodreads.com/quotes/527034-the-worst.
Guay, Paul and Stephen Mazur. Liar Liar. Directed by Tom Shadyac. Universal Studios, 1997.

Chapter Twelve
"Bernie Madoff: Who He Was, How His Ponzi Scheme Worked." Investopedia. Last modified March 29, 2023. https://www.investopedia.com/terms/b/bernard-madoff.asp.